Fostering Minority Access and Achievement in Higher Education

Richard C. Richardson, Jr.
Louis W. Bender

Fostering Minority Access and Achievement in Higher Education

The Role of Urban Community Colleges and Universities

Jossey-Bass Publishers
San Francisco • London • 1987

FOSTERING MINORITY ACCESS AND ACHIEVEMENT IN HIGHER EDUCATION
The Role of Urban Community Colleges and Universities
by Richard C. Richardson, Jr., and Louis W. Bender

 Jossey-Bass Inc., Publishers
433 California Street
San Francisco, California 94104
&
Jossey-Bass Limited
28 Banner Street
London EC1Y 8QE

Library of Congress Cataloging-in-Publication Data

Richardson, Richard C.
Fostering minority access and achievement in higher education.

(The Jossey-Bass higher education series)
Bibliography: p.
Includes index.
1. Minorities—Education (Higher)—United States.
2. Community colleges—United States. 3. Municipal universities and colleges—United States. 4. Students, Transfer of. 5. Degrees, Academic—United States.
I. Bender, Louis W. II. Title. III. Series.
LC3727.R53 1987 378'.052 87-45431
ISBN 1-55542-053-2 (alk. paper)

The project presented or reported herein was performed pursuant to grants from the Ford Foundation and the Office of Educational Research and Improvement/Department of Education (OERI/ED). However, the opinions expressed herein do not necessarily reflect the position or policy of the Ford Foundation or OERI/ED, and no official endorsement by either organization should be inferred.

Manufactured in the United States of America

The paper in this book meets the guidelines for permanence and durability of the Committee on Production Guidelines for Book Longevity of the Council on Library Resources.

JACKET DESIGN BY WILLI BAUM

FIRST EDITION

Code 8735

The Jossey-Bass
Higher Education Series

Contents

Preface

The inner cities of America, their minority student populations, and their public community colleges and public universities are the focus of this book. Cities have always held a strong attraction for the underprivileged, who migrate there in search of opportunity and in hope of a better life. Inner cities are disproportionately composed of racial and ethnic minorities, most of whom are from the lower socioeconomic strata. Education is their chief hope for upward socioeconomic mobility, and public community colleges and universities largely determine the extent to which their hopes are realized.

For more than two decades, policy leaders in the nation's more urban states have been concerned about higher education opportunities for inner-city residents. Their concern has been expressed in the development of new community college districts and urban universities as well as in the conversion and expansion of existing institutions. Opportunities for higher education in America's cities have been substantially broadened and strengthened, but the core of the problem remains; too few Hispanics and blacks are enrolled in baccalaureate programs and fewer still complete the requirements for a degree. As a result, Hispanics and blacks remain underrepresented in professional fields for which the baccalaureate degree is the gatekeeper. Although urban community colleges enroll disproportionate numbers of minority students, most pursue programs of study intended for job entry at the subprofessional and technical levels. The central question addressed in this book is why more of these students do not transfer and successfully complete baccalaureate programs. In our search for answers, we interviewed administrators and faculty members in urban universities in thirteen states. Urban community college administrators and faculty members in ten of these states contributed their insights as well. We also talked with coordinating board officials and collected research reports, position papers, and other available published evidence.

Background Information

This book draws on information from two overlapping studies, the first of which was carried out jointly by the authors and supported by the Ford Foundation (Richardson and Bender, 1986). The major questions addressed involve the policies, practices, and procedures at institutional or state levels that contribute to or discourage successful progression to the baccalaureate degree for students who begin their postsecondary educational experience in an urban community college. The study covered eight urban centers in eight different states and was conducted between January 1984 and November 1985. The methodology focused primarily on case studies but was augmented by a survey of students who had transferred successfully from a community college to a public university in each of the eight cities.

The second study, funded by the Office of Educational Research and Improvement (OERI) of the U.S. Department of Education in December 1985, was still in progress while this manuscript was being prepared. While the Ford study focused on urban community colleges with high enrollments of underrepresented minority students and the public universities to which the largest numbers of their students transferred, the OERI study selected ten universities with better than average records for graduating underrepresented minority students. Because an attempt was made to select states that had not participated in the Ford study, in order to broaden the data base (consistent with the intent of including those states that confer the highest number of degrees on minority students), only two urban universities, Florida International University and Temple University, participated in both studies.

The OERI study endeavors to account for the relative success of the selected universities in dealing with institutional practices, environmental influences (including but not limited to their relationships with adjacent community colleges), and state policy constraints. Six additional senior researchers are working with the authors of this volume in developing the institutional case studies that will form the body of a subsequent report.

This volume relies primarily on the Ford study for the content of Chapters Two through Eight, although available information from the OERI study was used in the process of triangulation. OERI data has been integrated into Chapters One, Nine, and Ten to extend the analysis, implications, and recommendations.

Who Should Read This Book

Fostering Minority Access and Achievement in Higher Education is addressed to policymakers at the state, city, and institutional levels. It will also provide administrators and faculty members in colleges and universities with insight into a problem many believe will be the most important issue facing higher education during the remainder of this century. Most of what we report will contain few surprises for those who work in urban settings on a daily basis. This work is not intended as an exposé; instead it is designed to provide a map of the forest for those who are intimately familiar with the trees.

Overview of the Contents

The first chapter discusses the dimensions of underrepresentation and relates them to the urban context, exploring the relationships between the public two-year colleges where most minorities initially enroll and the four-year institutions to which they must transfer in order to obtain the baccalaureate degree. We also provide additional information about the data bases used in developing the manuscript. Chapter Two describes the different and, in some ways conflicting, institutional cultures found in the community colleges and universities visited during the studies and explores the implications of these differences for interinstitutional cooperation and student transfer.

Chapter Three describes the range of educational and student support practices found in urban community colleges and relates these to strategies for overcoming barriers to successful transfer. Chapter Four explores the university policies and practices that contribute to or impede the progress of transfer students. In Chapter Five, the state environments are described as a means of distinguishing those variables institutions control from those imposed by the state educational system.

Chapter Six provides a profile of urban community college students as reflected in faculty members' descriptions of them and in autobiographical essays written by the students themselves. Chapter Seven summarizes observations from university faculty members concerning transfer students from community colleges, as well as the results of a survey of students who successfully transferred from an urban community college to a nearby urban university. Of particular interest are student responses to a question about possible improvements in the transfer process.

Chapter Eight presents advice from college administrators on overcoming obstacles to transfer. Chapter Nine provides answers to the research questions that organized our inquiries. Our analyses of student motives, preparation, progress, performance, and evaluations of their educational experiences are based on state and institutional research reports as well as on our survey and site visits. The final chapter interprets the evidence presented in the earlier chapters in terms of its implications for institutional and state policy.

Acknowledgments

The list of those who contributed to this manuscript is long indeed. Our Ford Foundation program officer, Alison

Bernstein, provided significant guidance at key points as well as flexibility when that virtue was needed. Through the National Center for Postsecondary Governance and Finance, the Office of Educational Research and Improvement provided the support necessary to continue and extend the Ford study as well as helpful comments in the latter stages of the project. The chief executive officers of institutions participating in the Ford study and their colleagues on the coordinating boards committed themselves to the study of issues that many consider sensitive and politically risky. The representatives they chose became our research colleagues and key informants as the study progressed. For their significant contributions we recognize each here: Jack Kinsinger, Arizona State University; Henry Moughamian, Chicago City Colleges; Margaret Faulwell, Chicago State University; Michael Wells, Cleveland State University; Jane Grosset, Community College of Philadelphia; Janet Smith, Cuyahoga Community College District; Richard McCrary, Dallas County Community College District; Scott Drakulich, Essex County College; Clair McElfresh, Florida International University; Jeffrey Lukenbill, Miami-Dade Community College; Marie Abrams, Phoenix College; Lincoln Lawrence, Rutgers University, Newark; Gwendolyn Stephenson, St. Louis Community College District; Betty Duvall, St. Louis Community College, Florissant Valley; William Law, St. Petersburg Junior College; Valaida Walker, Temple University; Julie Smith, University of Illinois, Chicago; Blanche Touhill, University of Missouri, St. Louis; Frank Spain, University of South Florida; Elwood Preiss, University of Texas, Arlington.

Researchers on the OERI project prepared preliminary drafts of the case studies of ten universities and provided their insights on minority degree achievement. In addition to the authors of this book, those conducting case studies for the OERI project include Patricia Crosson, University of Massachusetts, Amherst; Alfredo G. de los Santos, Jr., Maricopa Community Colleges; Howard Simmons, Middle States Association of Colleges and Schools; A. Wade Smith, Arizona State University; Robert Stout, Arizona State University; Gordon Van de Water, Augenblick, Van de Water Associates.

We also appreciate the efforts of those who coordinated

visits to state capitals. Particularly helpful during the Ford project were: Thomas Furlong, Florida Postsecondary Education Planning Commission; Robert Wallhaus, Illinois Board of Higher Education; Stephen Dougherty, Missouri Coordinating Board; Narcisa Jones, New Jersey State Board for Higher Education; Theresa Powell, Ohio Board of Regents; Warren Evans, Pennsylvania State Board of Education; Teresa Acosta, Texas Coordinating Board.

Graduate research associates at both our universities made important contributions; we especially acknowledge Ellie Strang, Naomi Johnson, and Susan Chalfant-Thomas.

June 1987

Richard C. Richardson, Jr.
Tempe, Arizona

Louis W. Bender
Tallahassee, Florida

The Authors

Richard C. Richardson, Jr., is associate director of the National Center for Postsecondary Governance and Finance and professor of educational leadership and policy studies at Arizona State University. He received his B.A. degree (1954) in education from Castleton State College, his M.A. degree (1958) in education from Michigan State University, and his Ph.D. degree (1963) in college administration from the University of Texas, Austin, where he was named distinguished graduate of the College of Education in 1982. He also holds an honorary doctorate from Lafayette College.

Richardson has served on the boards of the American Association of Community and Junior Colleges, the American Council on Education, and the American Association for Higher Education. His interest in organizational perspectives on access, equity, and educational outcomes is evident from his previous work, which includes *Literacy in the Open Access College* (1982), *Governance for the Two-Year College* (1972), and *The Two-Year College: A Social Synthesis* (1965).

Richardson was chair of the Department of Higher and

Adult Education at Arizona State University (1977–1984), founding president of Northampton County Area Community College in Bethlehem, Pennsylvania (1967–1977), and dean of instruction at St. Louis Community College, Forest Park (1964–1967).

Louis W. Bender is professor of higher education at Florida State University, where he also serves as director of the State and Regional Higher Education Center, which was established in 1970 with support from the W. K. Kellogg Foundation. He is active in system-level planning and policy studies related to governance, management, programming, and evaluation of postsecondary education. He received his B.A. degree (1950) in English from Moravian College and his M.A. degree (1952) in student personnel and his Ed.D. degree (1965) in college administration, both from Lehigh University.

Prior to assuming his present position, Bender served as the state director of community colleges in Pennsylvania during their formative years; he also served as assistant commissioner for higher education there. He is active at the state and national levels, serving as a member of the Board of Directors of the American Association of Community and Junior Colleges (AACJC) and as a member of the State Board for Independent Colleges and Universities in Florida. He received the Governor's Award for Excellence while in Pennsylvania and a distinguished service award from the Council of University and College Professors of AACJC.

Bender has coauthored numerous reports and books, including *The Politics of American Postsecondary Education* (1975) and *Governance for the Two-Year College* (1972).

Fostering Minority Access and Achievement in Higher Education

1

Understanding the Problem of Minority Underrepresentation in Higher Education Today

When equal opportunity in education first surfaced as a national concern, the term was defined in many settings as the ability to enroll in some postsecondary institution. But institutions are not equal in the types of opportunities they provide or in the resources at their disposal. It follows that the quality of an opportunity depends on the type of institution to which a student has access. And any arrangement that channels students to certain types of institutions as a function of race is suspect as an instrument for addressing traditional inequities in the educational opportunities available to minorities (Astin, 1982).

There is growing evidence that the policy decision made by many states in the 1960s to rely on community colleges as the primary access point for urban minorities has produced side effects that now threaten some of the hoped-for outcomes. Even though their participation increased dramatically during the sixties and seventies, there has been little change in economic and social class mobility for minorities because their curriculum choices have been so concentrated in the career and vocational areas. Minority attainment of associate degrees has been limited, and their subsequent progress to the baccalaureate remains relatively unchanged (Wilson, 1986).

Disproportionate Enrollments

Minorities are represented in two-year colleges at levels close to their proportional representation in the population (21.2 percent). They are underrepresented at the four-year level, where they constituted 14.5 percent in 1984. Hispanics have the highest concentration (54 percent) of students in two-year colleges. Blacks are less likely (43 percent) than Hispanics to attend two-year colleges. Whites are the least likely (36 percent) to attend community colleges (Wilson and Melendez, 1986). In California, community colleges enroll 40 percent of all high school graduates but 80 percent of all minority graduates (California Community Colleges, 1984).

Opportunities for Minorities in Community Colleges. The problem of disproportionate enrollments in community colleges might not be as serious if minority students were distributed randomly among the universe of two-year institutions. But this is not the case. Within community colleges, minority students are concentrated in a distinctive type of institution, the urban community college, where "50 percent to 70 percent of the high school students are minority" and "more than 50 percent drop out before they graduate" (Gittell, 1986, pp. 72-73). Among urban community colleges, segregation is increased by residential patterns and the absence of strategies for improving integration.

In Chicago, "black students are segregated in colleges which draw almost all of their students from a handful of all-black Chicago neighborhoods" (Orfield and others, 1984, p. ix). Blackwell (1982) refers to the growth of "newer predominantly black colleges," noting this as a phenomenon primarily of the two-year sector. Its consequence is to channel minority students into vocational programs "that all but preclude transfer to upper-division universities" (p. 37).

Urban community colleges, particularly those serving inner cities, admit large numbers of students who are very badly underprepared. They must serve them with resources that are frequently more constrained than those available to their suburban counterparts. The preoccupation with remediating from 60 to 95 percent of their entering students, along with the need to provide social services and to prepare their clientele for immediate employment, leaves them with little energy and few resources to offer challenging transfer programs to those who enroll with the ultimate intent of earning a baccalaureate degree.

Suburban community colleges in the Chicago area have more credibility with four-year institutions and experience greater success than urban community colleges in transferring their students (Orfield and others, 1984). In California, the well-publicized decline in the number of students transferring from community colleges is predominantly a phenomenon of the urban colleges. From 1979 to 1985 the number of students transferring from all community colleges in California to the University of California and California State University systems declined by 4 percent. The declines in numbers of students transferring from the Los Angeles and Peralta community college districts were 33 percent and 26 percent, respectively. Within these two large urban districts, losses were greatest among the predominantly minority colleges (California Postsecondary Education Commission, 1986).

Better prepared students in general, and white students in particular, attend suburban colleges in preference to inner-city institutions even when the latter are more convenient in terms of location. Most community college districts do not use attendance boundaries to regulate enrollment, and California, for example, has relaxed attendance restrictions across districts. While providing students with flexibility in deciding where to attend is meritorious from many perspectives, an unintended consequence is to increase segregation and to decrease academic competition in the inner-city institutions.

Minority students thus are concentrated in a subset of community colleges that along many dimensions do not provide the opportunities available in community colleges in general, much less those available in four-year institutions. This arrangement cannot, by any stretch of the imagination, be described as a strategy for promoting equal educational opportunity. The problem has many roots, not the least of which was the policy decision to address past discrimination in the distribution of educational opportunities through the cheap and efficient strategy of the commuter-oriented community college.

There are also several ways of approaching the undesirable side effects of this strategy. While analyzing ways to increase the flow of minorities from the community colleges where they are now overrepresented to the universities where they remain underrepresented is the primary focus of this book, it is not our intention to suggest that improving articulation is the only or even the most important step in addressing the challenge of providing equal educational opportunity. Four-year institutions have additional responsibilities beyond accepting the survivors of urban community colleges.

Underrepresentation in Four-Year Institutions. Urban four-year colleges, like their two-year counterparts, confront issues that are qualitatively different from those facing suburban schools. In particular, they are pulled by conflicting forces. Thus, they aspire to become more like traditional comprehensive or research universities while simultaneously providing programs that serve the best interests of their placebound, underrepresented, and often underprepared clientele. In many settings, the urban university was a response to the same pressures that created community colleges. Of the fifteen large urban universities in the South, all but one were created or became a freestanding unit of a state university during the last quarter century. Collectively, such institutions have contributed as much to minority access to education as have community colleges (Smartt, 1981).

The predominantly minority urban four-year institutions carry a disproportionate share of the responsibility for educating blacks and Hispanics. Typically, these institutions are classified as comprehensive rather than research universities. Their program offerings and their status as educational institutions are more limited than in predominantly white institutions in the same settings. Together with predominantly minority community colleges, minority universities may constitute "an interlocking system of educational stratification that treats minority and low-income students differently," so that the "higher education system does not operate to equalize opportunity but has powerful institutional features that tend to perpetuate separation and inequality" (Orfield and others, 1984, p. x).

Since blacks and Hispanics are underrepresented overall in four-year institutions, in addition to being concentrated among about fifty predominantly minority public institutions, it follows that available information significantly understates the degree of underrepresentation in the predominantly white four-year sector. This point has been well developed by Astin (1982), who found blacks significantly underrepresented in fifty-six out of sixty-five flagship universities and Hispanics similarly underrepresented in forty-nine of the same institutions. Urban universities do better than their flagship counterparts but substantially less well than adjacent inner-city community colleges.

There are differing approaches to calculating the degree of minority underrepresentation. Advocacy groups commonly compare the percentage of minorities in a state's population with their representation in a student body. A more restrictive and realistic approach compares representation in the student population with the proportion of minority students graduating from high schools in the primary service area. A third way of estimating underrepresentation involves comparing university enrollments with qualified high school graduates (those who completed the necessary courses with an appropriate grade point average) and those who become qualified through attendance at a community college within the primary service area.

Universities also employ different strategies for reducing the degree of minority underrepresentation, however it is calculated. A research report characterizes these alternatives as the traditional, mediation, and intervention approaches (Whiteley and Lacy, 1985). The traditional approach focuses on competing for a limited number of qualified minority candidates. A mediation approach adds, to the attempt to recruit qualified minority candidates, special admissions criteria for minorities (in effect, it provides a waiver of regular admission requirements), summer bridge programs, and academic support services, including remediation and tutoring. The intervention approach attempts to expand the pool of qualified minority candidates through working directly with junior and senior high schools and with community colleges to provide early advising, college awareness, role models, and instructional enhancement.

Minorities and the Baccalaureate Degree. Up to this point, our discussion has focused on participation in the educational process as the measure of underrepresentation. But participation is not an end in itself. So it is also necessary to examine the question of how many winners there are among those who participate. Of equal interest is the question of which institutions contribute the most to minority degree production and under what circumstances.

A relatively small number of schools account for most of the baccalaureate degrees awarded to minorities. Of the 1,658 baccalaureate institutions reported in 1978-79, 22 percent (362) accounted for 82 percent of the bachelor's degrees awarded to blacks and 80 percent of those awarded to Hispanics. The majority of institutions awarded fewer than 50 degrees to any minority group in that year. Most degrees were awarded to minority students in urban settings (74 percent) by public institutions (75.7 percent).

Of the 362 institutions awarding most of the bachelor's degrees earned by minority students, 92 (25 percent) served predominantly minority populations (Deskins, 1983). For blacks, predominantly black colleges awarded 34 percent of all black undergraduate degrees in 1981 and more than 40 percent of all degrees for blacks in agriculture, computer sciences, biology, mathematics, physical sciences, and social sciences (College Entrance Examination Board, 1985). The case for the effectiveness and continuing importance of traditionally black colleges has been forcefully stated (Fleming, 1984). At the same time, it does not seem likely that such institutions will assume a larger share of the responsibility for reducing discrepancies between minority and nonminority degree achievement. Between 1976 and 1981, traditionally black institutions experienced an 8 percent decline in their share of the degrees awarded to black students. Since 1980 enrollments at these institutions have declined by 3 percent. Enrollments at the forty-one traditionally black four-year public colleges have also become increasingly diverse under the influence of *Adams* v. *Richardson* (Wilson and Melendez, 1986).

Among urban institutions not classified as traditionally black, graduation rates vary widely as a function of admission practices, enrollment status of the student body (full time versus part time), institutional character (multicultural versus predominantly white), and the period of time over which the rates were calculated. The following five examples illustrate the effects of these characteristics. (Graduation rates, however, are also influenced by institutional practices and state policies—variables that receive focused attention elsewhere in this volume.)

Within the California State University system, over two-thirds of new black admits and one-half of new Hispanic admits do not meet regular admission criteria. The five-year graduation rate for black regular admits is 12.5 percent and for special admits 7 percent. For Hispanics, the comparable figures are 19.3 percent and 4 percent. The same figures for white admits are 32.6 percent and 15.8 percent (California State University, 1986). The very low completion rates reported for this system are a function of admission practices (large numbers of minority students are admitted outside of regular admission requirements) and the short duration of the study (part-time students typically require longer than five years to complete the bachelor's degree).

The City University of New York (CUNY) studied completion rates in its senior colleges using a similar way of categorizing students but extending the study over eleven years (Lavin, Murtha, and Kaufman, 1984). In the case of regular admits, the graduation rate for blacks was 59 percent, for Hispanics 48 percent, and for whites 59 to 67 percent. The rates for open admission students were blacks 40 percent, Hispanics 31 percent, and whites 40 to 48 percent. CUNY is more multicultural than the California State University system and includes several predominantly minority institutions. The higher completion rate for CUNY also reflects the longer duration of the study.

The University of California, Los Angeles (UCLA), is a highly selective, multicultural institution populated largely by full-time students. Because of the attractiveness of the university to minority candidates, it makes only limited use of special admission criteria in meeting its commitment to achieve a representative student body. At UCLA, the five-year graduation rate for black regular admits is 46 percent, for Hispanics 38 percent, and for whites 60 percent. The comparable five-year rates for special admits are blacks, 16 percent, Hispanics, 12 percent, and whites, 36 percent (University of California, Los Angeles, 1986).

Memphis State University operates under strict guidelines and monitoring procedures as a result of a court decree that resolved more than a decade of litigation over desegregation of the state's higher education systems. In 1981, blacks represented 19 percent of the university's first-time freshmen. In 1984-85, blacks represented 14 percent of the baccalaureate recipients (Desegregation Monitoring Committee, 1986). Placing as much emphasis on graduation as on participation has helped Memphis State move from a segregated institution in 1958 to a state and national leader in the production of black baccalaureates.

A research study from the University of Missouri, St. Louis (Avakian, MacKinney, and Allen, 1983), demonstrates one additional facet of the degree attainment process for minorities. For first-time freshmen, the proportion of blacks who graduated or were still enrolled after seven years was 19 percent while the comparable figure for whites was 39 percent. For transfer students during the same period, there were no significant differences in the percentages of white and black students graduated or retained.

Several observations emerge from the study of these and similar reports on graduation rates disaggregated by race. First, it is clear that there is merit in the arguments of those who are concerned about the extent to which institutional differences are submerged in national data bases. Second, the wide variance in results being achieved by institutions may be due in part to circumstances over which these institutions have limited control; at the same time, however, variables that the institutions can control appear to make a difference. Third, the results being achieved by four-year institutions with the minority students they recruit as native freshmen are not so outstanding in most settings as to justify disregarding the potential contribution of urban community colleges to the production of minority baccalaureates. While the evidence is mixed, some indicators suggest that it is an advantage for underprepared minority students to begin their collegiate work in a community college (Breneman and Nelson, 1981). It is to this possibility that we now turn our attention.

Articulation: The Urban Connection

Freedom of movement among institutions having significantly different missions, program emphases, and admission criteria for entering freshmen is a central premise undergirding state systems of higher education in the United States as they have evolved during the era of open access. Transfer from community colleges to major public universities represents an important avenue to the baccalaureate in most states with large numbers of minority students. In Florida, 76 percent of the minority students begin their education in a community college. In 1983, more than 43,000 students transferred from Florida community colleges to public universities, where they represented 42 percent of all state university system undergraduates (Florida Board of Regents, 1985). In California, 50,000 students transfer annually from community colleges to the two public university systems (California Postsecondary Education Commission, 1986).

We have already noted that minority students are better represented in high school graduating classes than in postsecondary institutions. And among postsecondary institutions they are disproportionately concentrated in urban community colleges. From community colleges, they commonly transfer at rates below those of their white counterparts. In the words of a California State University report (1986, p. 21), "The educational pipeline for minority students is one of inordinately diminishing percentages."

There is no dearth of information about articulation and

transfer. Two recent publications (Kintzer and Wattenbarger, 1985; Richardson and Bender, 1985) summarize the extensive literature available. Most reports concentrate on one of two areas. The first involves studies of student persistence and performance. In general, such studies demonstrate that transfer remains an important, if proportionately diminished, part of the community college mission. Those who transfer after completing a reasonable number of credits continue to perform in ways not significantly different from those who began their education in four-year colleges when aptitude and high school performance are held constant. A second genre of articulation report focuses on coordinating board policies that were adopted to encourage cooperation among two- and four-year institutions within a state system. As in the case of persistence studies, the sense of these reports is positive. Most states have adopted policies and guidelines designed to smooth the process of transfer for students who begin their postsecondary careers in a community college.

But the literature can be deceiving. State policies and guidelines must be interpreted and applied at the institutional level. Frequently policies are advisory rather than binding. Relationships among key administrators, the attitudes of faculty, and the magnitude of administrative bureaucracies influence the degree to which coordinating board intentions become operational in the transfer experience. Persistence studies are rarely disaggregated by race. Where such information is available, there is evidence that transfer in urban settings may be qualitatively and quantitatively different from the suburban experience (California Postsecondary Education Commission, 1986).

How Data for the Study Were Gathered

Much has been written about possible causes of the discrepancies in baccalaureate achievement between blacks and Hispanics, on the one hand, and their white and Asian counterparts, on the other. It is often suspected that these discrepancies result from federal financial aid policies and the influence of institutional variables on underrepresented minorities who, as previously noted, are more likely to attend community colleges than their nonminority counterparts. But while correlational analyses of large data bases are valuable in furnishing insights into the strength of relationships among contributing variables, they fall short of describing the interplay of state policies and institutional practices that influence degree achievement. Moreover, determining that attendance at a community college is related to the likelihood of dropping out before attaining a baccalaureate degree provides little substantive guidance to states that rely on two-year colleges as a central part of their strategy for promoting equal opportunity. Neither does such information provide much assistance to those minority students for whom the community college is and will remain in the foreseeable future their primary or sole access to higher education.

This study was designed to build on the existing base of knowledge about degree achievement among minority students by looking in depth at policies and practices in major urban areas that were selected because of their importance to the national scene in the education of blacks and Hispanics and because of their reliance on articulation between two- and four-year institutions to provide educational opportunities to students traditionally underrepresented in state higher education systems.

The evidence gathered during the preparation of this manuscript spans two different studies that involved a total of thirteen states. Visits were made to community colleges in Los Angeles, Oakland, and New York as part of the development of a proposal to the Ford Foundation that was funded in January of 1984. The Ford study focused on community college–university pairs in eight metropolitan areas: Chicago, Cleveland, Dallas, Miami, Newark, Philadelphia, Phoenix, and St. Louis, as well as on their respective state coordinating boards (Richardson and Bender, 1986). A follow-up study funded by the Office of Educational Research and Improvement (OERI) of the U.S. Department of Education in December of 1985 added universities in Albuquerque, Detroit, El Paso, Los Angeles, and Memphis.

Site visits were made to institutions and state coordinating boards in five of the ten states that graduate the most black baccalaureates: New York, California, Illinois, Texas, and Florida. The five states not included–North Carolina, Louisiana, Alabama, Virginia, and Mississippi–rely on traditionally black institutions rather than linkages between two- and four-year institutions in urban centers for the larger proportion of their minority degree production. Nine of the top ten states in the production of Hispanic baccalaureates–Texas, California, New York, Florida, New Mexico, New Jersey, Illinois, Arizona, and Pennsylvania–were also included (Deskins, 1983).

The primary goal of the site visits was to describe state policies and institutional practices as these appeared to influence student persistence in pursuit of the baccalaureate. Site visits were planned in consultation with institutional representatives, who arranged appointments and collected relevant documents. Prior to each visit, site representatives were provided with a brief written statement of the purpose of the study and a copy of the interview guides. These documents were shared with institutional staff members to give them an opportunity to prepare for the interview and to encourage them to bring copies of relevant papers or forms. Site visits were augmented by essays written by community college freshmen describing their background, current status, and future aspirations, as well as by surveys of a representative sample of students who had transferred successfully from community colleges to universities participating in the Ford study. Institutional representatives contributed to the design of the survey instrument. They also reviewed a draft of the project report and assisted in developing the policy implications.

Interview data from the site visits, surveys, and essays were triangulated with state and institutional studies of student flow and with the literature on equal opportunity, minority student achievement, and articulation. Table 1 provides an overview of the data sources, methodology, and chronology of the studies.

The intent of the design was to provide some reasonable balance among the five types of information suggested by Murphy (1980) as critical to the conduct of field investigations. Through focused interviewing, observation, document analysis, and a survey, we sought information about:

Table 1. Description of Data Sources.

Data Sources	*Nature of Data*	*Purpose*
Site visits to community colleges in Los Angeles, Oakland, and New York (Sept. 1983 to Feb. 1984)	Structured interviews with faculty members and administrators; document collection	Policies and practices; student preparation and achievement; relationships with adjacent university
Ford site visits to community colleges and universities in eight cities (Sept. 1984 to Dec. 1984)	Structured interviews with faculty members and administrators; document collection	Transfer-related policies and practices; student preparation and achievement; cooperation
OERI site visits to universities (Oct. 1986 to Dec. 1986)	Structured interviews with faculty members and administrators; document collection	Baccalaureate achievement by minority students
Ford site visits to coordinating boards in eight states (Feb. 1985 to May 1985)	Structured interviews with coordinating board officers	State policies and initiatives related to transfer and financial aid
OERI site visits to coordinating boards (Oct. 1986 to Dec. 1986)	Structured interviews with coordinating board officers; document collection	State policies and initiatives related to baccalaureate achievement and financial aid
Essays written by community college students in beginning English classes (Jan. 1985 to June 1985)	Content analysis of essays coded by race, institution, and nature of response	Student home environment, reasons for attending a community college, and future plans
Survey responses from representative samples of students who transferred from a community college to a university in the Ford study (Feb. 1985 to May 1985)	Computer file of individual responses to a twenty-four-item survey coded by race, institution, and academic major	Timing of transfer decisions; evaluations of community colleges and universities; suggestions for improving the transfer process
Document files (continuous)	Publications; research reports; position papers; fact books	Corroborate interviews; quantitative data on student outcomes

1. Context—information about the state, community, and organizational settings of urban community colleges and universities
2. Essential program elements—types of programs, support services, and administrative arrangements that must be understood to draw inferences about the impact of the transfer function on minority degree achievement
3. Program evolution—the period of time during which changes have influenced current outcomes
4. Strengths and weaknesses of current outcomes—the current outcomes regarded as strengths and those regarded as problematic
5. Areas of improvement—policy decisions at given levels that would emphasize program strengths and reduce weaknesses

The Study in Perspective

Urban community colleges share some similarities with their public university neighbors. Both deal with economic deprivation, high attrition, failing school systems, and limited institutional funding. There are similar institutional problems: confusing missions, overvaluing traditional ways at the expense of community needs, undervaluing institutional cooperation, and failing to communicate (Cafferty and Spangenberg, 1981). Gittell (1986) suggests that urban community colleges and urban universities may be more like one another than either is like its suburban counterpart.

But there are also some important differences. Universities serving an urban clientele are perhaps best described as American universities in urban settings. While they reflect their locale by providing programs that serve the basic needs of an urban clientele, they are concerned about the image that accompanies serving nontraditional students. Their urban mission is more commonly expressed through curricula and research that focus on urban topics and problems than through programs or service designed to directly affect the conditions of urban living. Their professors find it difficult to accommodate the cultural differences found among students (Rudnick, 1983).

Opportunities to earn a baccalaureate degree for the majority of minority students who begin their postsecondary education in an urban community college are largely dependent on the relationship that exists between it and the adjacent public university to which most of them transfer. One purpose of our studies was to describe those aspects of urban community college and university cultures that determine the effectiveness of the transfer process, and we also examined the pressures for cooperation that arise from coordinating board policies. Our intent was to develop evidence about existing arrangements as a means of identifying strategies through which the transfer process might be improved for all students attending urban institutions. Our underlying assumption was that such strategies would benefit minority students disproportionately because of their overrepresentation in urban colleges.

Several terms used throughout this manuscript require definition. When the term *minorities* is used without elaboration, we refer to blacks and Hispanics. *Urban community colleges* are campuses of the major metropolitan district serving one of the cities that we visited while carrying out research for this book. Among urban community colleges, we distinguish between *inner-city colleges,* that is, those campuses in each district with the highest minority enrollments, and *more suburban campuses,* which have predominantly white or multicultural enrollments. Institutions with relatively balanced student populations involving two or more racial groups have a *multicultural* enrollment. *Suburban community colleges* are those serving the residential areas ringing the cities we studied. They have predominantly white enrollments unless otherwise noted.

Urban universities are public four-year institutions located in the same cities as the urban community colleges studied. They were selected for the Ford study because they received the largest number of transfer students sent to any four-year institution by participating urban community colleges. Urban universities in the OERI study were selected because they graduate a higher than average proportion of minority students. *Comprehensive universities* have few or no doctoral programs and concentrate primarily on teaching and service. *Research universities* have as their highest priority expanding their doctoral programs and sponsored research.

The process of gathering evidence about the influence of relationships between urban community colleges and urban universities on minority degree attainment was guided by the following questions:

1. How many of the students who enroll in urban community colleges have objectives and previous academic experience that suggest that transfer to a four-year institution would be a reasonable expectation?
2. Among those students with the necessary objectives and preparation, how many actually transfer and at what stage of their academic careers? How well represented are minorities among these urban transfers?
3. How do transfers from urban community colleges perform at major receiving institutions? Are there differences between the performance or persistence of minority transfer students and that of transfer students in general?
4. What strengths and weaknesses do urban transfer students attribute to their previous academic experience? Are there differences between minority transfers and their white counterparts?
5. How do urban community colleges contribute to baccalaureate achievement by their students? In what ways could their contributions be enhanced?
6. How do urban universities contribute to baccalaureate achievement by students who transfer from urban community colleges? In what ways could their contributions be strengthened?
7. How do state policies and leadership contribute to baccalaureate achievement by urban minorities? In what ways could their contributions be enhanced?

There are also dangers in treating ethnic minorities as homogeneous groups. Cubans are more likely to attend college and to have higher family incomes than other Hispanic subgroups (Santos, 1986). They also score differently on achievement tests (Pennock-Roman, 1986). Middle-class blacks perform in ways similar to their white counterparts; that is, they achieve academic records in high school that qualify them to attend the most selective universities. As this chapter was being written, there was a lively debate in progress at UCLA between staff members in the Academic Advancement Program, which serves minority undergraduates, and the university administration. Program staffers are geared to working with Third World students admitted under special criteria. Increasingly, underrepresented minorities at UCLA meet regular admission criteria and come from upper-middle-class backgrounds.

Because this is a book about urban minorities, we have chosen to exclude Native Americans from our discussion. While this group is also underrepresented in higher education, the institutions that enroll most Native Americans were not for the most part the ones contributing to the body of information on which this book was based. Also, while Asian students are an important urban minority, particularly in West Coast cities, they are not an underrepresented minority. And regardless of how underrepresentation is measured, it is obvious that blacks and Hispanics do not currently experience access to higher education in the same way as Asians and whites.

Conclusion

The problem of minority underrepresentation among baccalaureate degree holders is a problem of access to four-year institutions rather than one of participation in a college experience. Access to four-year institutions for almost half of all minority students currently participating in higher education requires transfer from a two-year to a four-year institution. Among the persistent obstacles that transfer students from nontraditional backgrounds must overcome to achieve their bachelor's degree are adverse demographic and economic trends, lack of dollars to support necessary programs, staff deficiencies in skills or attitudes, community apathy and even hostility, unhealthy competition among institutions for resources and students, outdated institutional missions, public misperception of institutional purpose, and organizational inflexibilities (American Association of State Colleges and Universities, 1979). Significantly, the majority of these variables are under institutional control and reflect administrative priorities rather than instructional deficiencies.

No one believes that more than two centuries of segregation and discrimination will be erased in one generation by improved access to baccalaureate education. Past practices and their present correlates in the form of poverty, unemployment, segregated housing patterns, and differential access to public school education should not, however, become a justification for continuing neglect of those variables that colleges and universities do influence. In the aggregate, such variables have the potential for reducing at least part of the gap between minority and nonminority degree achievement.

In building the case for improved articulation among two- and four-year colleges in urban settings as one strategy for addressing current inequities in the distribution of baccalaureate degree opportunities, we have relied most heavily on what we were told by administrators and faculty members in the institutions and state coordinating board offices we visited. Wherever possible we have supplemented their statements with the research reports, position papers, and related written materials that came to our attention during the studies. But in the final analysis this book represents our informed judgment about the root causes of minority underrepresentation in postsecondary education and possible strategies for addressing this complex and important social issue that seems likely to dominate much of the discussion on higher education during the next two decades. Throughout the book we have avoided attributing practices or outcomes to specific institutions or states except where our information sources were in the public domain. The decision to avoid attribution was based on the assumption that it would improve candor and add to the chances of obtaining the level of institutional cooperation necessary to the type of study we wanted to do.

2

Barriers to Cooperation Between Community Colleges and Universities

Community colleges and universities represent different cultures in terms of their belief systems and the behavior that gives these beliefs meaning. Waetjen and Muffo (1983) have suggested a continuum to describe the array of institutional missions found in urban settings. At one extreme are those institutions that take as their model the residential research university and accept their urban location as a matter of coincidence. At the other extreme are socially involved institutions that function in part as welfare agencies and attempt to improve the conditions of urban life for those who attend them. In the middle are transitional institutions that retain their academic character without isolating themselves from the conditions that affect the people who share their urban location.

While the Waetjen and Muffo continuum was developed to describe the role of urban universities, it also provides a useful framework for distinguishing between urban community colleges and urban universities. Inner-city community colleges are socially involved institutions whose concern for their students is reflected in a wide array of social services, as well as in a willingness to adapt academic programs and policies to the needs of their inner-city students. Comprehensive universities, especially those that serve a predominantly minority clientele, are torn between their desire to pursue traditional academic values and their commitment to a student population that differs in important ways from those best able to take advantage of traditional approaches. The frame of reference for research universities is not their urban setting but what Parsons and Platt (1973) refer to as the core university values of graduate study and research. The needs and concerns of their urban setting are secondary although they are not completely ignored.

The importance of these differences in organizational culture to the educational opportunities provided to students in urban settings can scarcely be overstated. According to Schein (1985), the term *culture* describes the deeper assumptions and beliefs shared by members of an organization. Assumptions and beliefs represent learned responses by groups to the need to survive in an external environment and to achieve internal integration. Organizational culture is thus the product of shared experiences that lead to a view of the world and the organization's place in it. Culture not only involves technology and visible behavior patterns but extends to values and basic assumptions about human nature, human relationships, and human activity as well. We believe with Schein that institutional structure and attitudes are "artifacts of culture" (p. 33). In groups that have had enough history to develop a culture, that culture becomes all-encompassing. Most urban community colleges and universities have now been in existence long enough and have experienced enough stability to meet the conditions for establishing a culture. The organizational cultures they have developed are a function of their leadership since, as Schein has pointed out, culture and leadership are in reality two sides of the same coin.

It follows from this analysis that the culture produced by one leadership style can be altered by another. This suggestion frames one of the key objectives of this book. Helping leaders of urban community colleges, urban universities, and state systems understand the impact of the cultures that they have helped to create on the educational opportunities of students in urban settings can provide those leaders with insights into the changes necessary to improve baccalaureate opportunities for minority students.

Thus, improving opportunities for urban transfer students involves helping them to adjust to two different kinds of institutions, each with its own set of values and basic assumptions. There are two complicating problems, both of which lend themselves to institutional intervention. The first involves the absence of friends or relatives who have had experience with higher education and who understand and support the sacrifices necessary for its attainment. The second involves the lack of understanding among community colleges and universities of the differences between their cultures. Accompanying this lack of understanding is an absence of respect for the differences in attitudes and behavior that these cultures produce. As a result, neither does as much as it could to help students understand or adjust to the other's culture.

The concept that community colleges and universities represent different cultures is not new. Jencks and Riesman (1968) described community colleges as "antiuniversity colleges" and concluded that they did not represent an alternative path to the top but rather a safety valve that permitted universities to pursue their priorities without unleashing a populist backlash. Weiss (1985) suggests that black students in an urban community college are caught between two worlds, a situation that ensures that most of them will return to the ghetto streets.

While most observers reject Karabel's (1986) continuing criticism of community colleges as institutions that reinforce rather than interrupt existing patterns of social relationships, the issue deserves continuing attention in urban areas where community colleges are the major point of entry for upwardly aspiring minority populations. And the concept of class or culture is particularly useful in interpreting the differences that we observed between the community colleges and the urban universities that participated in our studies. The ways in which urban universities and community colleges view themselves and each other have significant implications for understanding the barriers that urban students must surmount in their pursuit of the baccalaureate degree.

Urban Community Colleges in Context

Community college administrators clearly perceived their mission differently than did their university counterparts. One district chancellor characterized the role of a community college in an urban area as "providing access understood in different ways. Economic access, of course, but sociological access as well to people who had never thought of going to college." He mentioned new immigrants and Mexicans from rural backgrounds as individuals who should be encouraged to utilize the college for personal reasons even if they had no intention of earning a degree. "As institutions, we get people inside the door!" This chancellor, more direct than most, made it clear that he was not convinced of the importance of the baccalaureate degree to urban students. From his perspective, urban community colleges were created for people who were not candidates for a bachelor's degree.

The chief executive officer of another district disagreed:

> The academic transfer function must be the primary cornerstone of the community college's mission. While there is a break between the high school and postsecondary institutions, we must recognize the continuum of the baccalaureate program made up of the community college's lower-division work and the upper-division programs of the university. The complexity of fitting or being part of that program continuum is created by the university's calling for quite different and diverse elements among the various transfer majors, which serves as an inhibitor to the student's orderly progress to the baccalaureate degree.

The leaders of urban community colleges, especially those

campuses serving a predominantly minority population, thus were mixed in their reactions to the importance of transfer even though most understood clearly the limitations that their students would have to overcome if they were to benefit from baccalaureate-oriented work. As one campus president noted:

> Transfer is one of our highest priorities at this time; the college can transform the lives of people in dramatic ways. It provides fulfillment for minorities who have not had access to upward mobility previously.

But overshadowing the more idealistic aspirations was the concern for enrollments. As another president noted:

> The current priority of this campus is to try to figure out ways to cope with a forecasted continuing decline in enrollment; [since] the whole district has been geared to grow, the impact on budgeting of the current decline is a very major concern.

Apart from enrollment problems, the characteristics of students attending inner-city campuses posed formidable problems for those who advocated an emphasis on the baccalaureate degree. The president of one inner-city college who had previously served in the same capacity in a suburban community college in a different state commented on the contrast. In the suburban college, the student body was middle class and came predominantly from families who had been exposed to higher education and valued its outcomes. Inner-city students came predominantly from backgrounds where higher education was neither understood nor advocated:

> There is a conflict in the value and cultural perspectives of our college faculty and the student body we serve which is not always consciously acknowledged or even understood on the part of many faculty and staff.

She believed that the nontraditional students attending her present college required a quite different approach from that used in her previous institution:

> The faculty here are prone to quest for and even practice the traditional academic values and approaches, but what is worse is the tendency of some faculty to inappropriately apply dual standards in sympathy for the plight of the student, thereby further complicating the problem.

In response to the pressure of enrollment declines and an underprepared student clientele, inner-city colleges have undergone significant transformations during the past decade. One campus president described her downtown college, which served a predominantly minority clientele, as a victim of its location. It had been the original campus of a multicollege district. As new campuses were established, its academic transfer population declined, and suburban campuses increasingly came to serve the middle-class clientele that had previously attended the inner-city campus. As a result, her college now emphasized career programs and community services with few or no programs for transfer students. She observed:

> All bus routes converge in front of the college. Those students who come during the traditional hours are from the socioeconomic group that must use bus transportation rather than automobiles.

This reality was reflected in the college's fact book, which reported that over 60 percent of the students were classified as below the poverty level. Contributing to the trend toward more emphasis on career preparation, the college has moved to vocational settings in business, industry, and government as the "markets" toward which programming should be directed. One-hour "flex courses" designated for saturation in a specific content area, along with outreach classes held in corporate buildings, were the priority areas for educational programming. Despite these significant changes in educational emphasis, however, the president reported no systematic assessment of student goals or student outcomes. The university to which students from this college most commonly transferred did not grant transfer credit for the flex courses.

The more suburban campuses of multicampus districts (those colleges that serve lower percentages of minority students) perceived themselves as different from (and most commonly superior to) those that served predominantly minority populations. One administrator observed, "At [our college] we are the top of the line academically; our students who have gone on rate the quality of teaching here as higher than at their transfer institutions." At the same time, such administrators were not blind to the social implications of the differences in the student populations they served:

> The civil rights charges that our district colleges were deliberately placed to encourage segregation are not true from my experience. They were designed to promote access; the fact that they are segregated is a function of city housing patterns.

Most urban community college districts did not set out to achieve racially balanced campuses. Their policies, with exceptions for some of the more expensive programs, provided for similar offerings on all campuses; hence, geography became a determinant of the clientele served. Low-income students consistently identified proximity and cost as their most important reasons for attending a community college. Thus, the district policies ended up producing heavily segregated campuses because of the residential patterns of the cities where they were located.

While the intent of offering comprehensive programs in each location may have been to provide equal access, student mobility patterns produced evidence that students did not always perceive equity as the outcome of this strategy. Students living close to an inner-city campus who could afford transportation costs and had high aspirations frequently made the trip to a more suburban campus where they believed they would get a better education. Both inner-city and more suburban campus administrators reported this pattern for the better prepared minority students. One administrator observed:

> Many college students travel for considerable distances to attend the suburban campus despite the absence of convenient public transportation and the fact that that particular campus has the worst physical facilities of any in the district. It is seen as the top of the line, and our better students who can afford going there will do so.

Faculty at the inner-city colleges were also aware of the differences between their institutions and their more suburban sister colleges. In one district, where a more suburban campus enjoyed the luxury of preregistering 80 percent of its students and being able to require a writing sample during the preregistration assessment process, envy was in evidence from a dean of the inner-city college, who observed:

> At the extreme, our students walk by and see a sign on the college marquee, "Registration Going on Now," and they turn and say, "I guess I'll go to college," and in they walk. Their preparation is just about as limited as their planning for college.

The procedures through which available funds were allocated to the individual colleges within a district had an important influence on the operations of inner-city campuses. Typically, most resources were distributed on the basis of enrollments, with incremental changes reflecting routine fluctuations in the costs of doing business. While district administration in theory gave the campus considerable discretion in the expenditure of budgeted funds, in practice this amounted to charging the campus head with the responsibility for meeting relatively fixed costs that seemed always to increase at a faster rate than the annual budget authorization. Discretionary funds were scarce and tightly controlled at the district level. When individual campuses competed for discretionary funds, there was a marked tendency among senior administrators to favor proposals that emphasized the use of technology rather than the hiring of new staff, and to support establishing new programs over strengthening the old. This tendency helped to explain the fairly common perception at the campus level of underfunding for the task of working with underprepared students while at the district level there was the perception of adequate or even generous funding.

In the resource allocation process, attempts were generally made to provide some protection for those inner-city campuses that were experiencing a drop in enrollment. But it was difficult to describe such protection as part of a plan to provide differential consideration to the campus serving the most disadvantaged students. Rather, it seemed more an expedient stemming from contractual obligations and political necessity. At the time of the study, planning was in a state of flux for most of the districts because of the need to adjust from an era of growth to the present one of no growth or decline. The environment called for broad-based strategic planning, and most of the districts were moving in this direction, albeit reluctantly and often with the hope that a new emphasis on marketing would renew the growth cycle.

While the impact of funding constraints on programs and services seemed limited, some consequences did have an impact on students pursuing baccalaureate work. Courses with limited enrollments were not offered as frequently; hence, many sequential and prerequisite academic courses were available only in certain terms or when a minimum number of students were registered. This restriction fell heaviest on transfer offerings in the inner-city colleges that minority students were most likely to attend. Perhaps the absence or irregular availability of academic courses requiring prerequisites accounted for some of the student migration toward the more suburban campuses.

While many district and campus leaders believed that community colleges should be first and most importantly academic institutions, most inner-city colleges have moved far along the continuum toward a social welfare role. Extensive support services have been established in an effort to cope with the wide range of problems endemic to inner-city student populations. Financial assistance, child care, and health services address important student needs. But the emphasis on these services and the tendency for faculty to adapt academic expectations to student performance combine to dilute academic standards and reduce expectations for student achievement.

If urban community colleges are not all things to all people, they are nonetheless the most important hope for their urban clientele for breaking the cycle of poverty and despair. At the same time, districts must maintain a favorable revenue picture by offering courses that produce more revenues than they use. The tempting role of social welfare provider shapes the values and attitudes of faculty members and administrators as well as their expectations for student achievement. The extensive services, supportive environments, and lack of rigor in course work described in greater detail in Chapter Three represent logical responses. But student retention in the absence of progress toward meeting academic goals places some inner-city colleges perilously close to becoming custodial institutions where keeping students enrolled by preventing them from failing takes priority over challenging them to succeed.

Urban Universities and Their Environment

Urban universities, particularly those pursuing status as research universities as distinct from those that had already arrived, were also subject to conflicting forces. State policymakers believed that these institutions should devote a considerable part of their effort to serving the urban areas where they were situated. Teaching and service, however, interfered with efforts to achieve major research status. In keeping with the desire of their institutions to become major research universities, faculty members preferred to have the best and brightest students in their classes. But the reality of their urban existence meant that most students came from surrounding schools, many of which were inadequate by most standards. As a result, students were less well prepared and more occupationally oriented than the image of a research institution suggested they should have been.

There was inevitably the question of whether urban universities should pursue an urban mission or assume major research status and merely be located in the urban area. Among the universities in this study, about half were in each camp on this issue.

The most socially involved discussion of urban mission was provided by the president of a comprehensive university serving a predominantly minority student body who believed that his institution "should impact on the community. It should be a resource in terms of dealing with such urban problems as energy, economic development, and even street gangs." He also emphasized the teaching mission of the institution and its responsibility to recruit and educate students who lived in the urban area surrounding the college. Finally, he noted a number of cultural and community service activities that he felt should be offered; these ranged from free noncredit courses such as income tax preparation to family planning and consumer economics. In many values and priorities, this university seemed closer to the community college than to the research university. Nevertheless, it placed emphasis upon its role as an academic rather than a social institution, a distinction not always clear for the inner-city community college.

A vice-chancellor at an urban research university provided a very different answer to the same question. While acknowledging that the institution could not separate itself from the metropolitan area, he pointed out:

> That does not mean that this place is a high-class trade school. There are certain components that are absolute in the university, regardless of its location—the arts and sciences and the quantitative disciplines. One cannot imagine a university without a program in physics or efforts in human help and the fine arts, which are absolutely critical in urban society. Outside the core components are the professional programs in concentric circles.

He noted that identifying programs with the community did not mean that the theoretical or knowledge generation values should be sacrificed in the interests of utilitarianism. When asked if there were dynamic tensions between community needs and university responses, his answer was, "You're damned right!"

The president of a university serving a growing and dynamic metropolitan area spoke of the external pressures from the power structure for his university to move from serving the inner-city expectations of an urban institution to serving those of suburban interest groups in order to become one of the flagship universities in that state. He observed that his faculty and administrators lived in the suburbs and embraced the quest for flagship status. This university, with the support of economic developers, as well as of local, state, and national politicians, concentrated its energies and resources on high-tech research and development, medical education, engineering, and business. Little energy and few resources remained for the student and academic support services required to serve the urban minority student.

Despite important differences among the universities we visited in terms of mission, priorities, level of maturity, and state environments, they evidenced a common concern for academic values that distinguished them from the community colleges that shared their urban environment. For many of these institutions, the fiscal environment has been constrained during the past decade. This may form a brief interlude in the history of each state's flagship university, but it constitutes almost half the total life-span for many of the newer urban universities. Fiscally constrained environments have produced competition between the better established public universities and their newer urban counterparts for programs, faculty members, students, and facilities. Where the competition has not been closely controlled by a system governing board or a state coordinating board, newer urban universities have seldom emerged as victors.

Securing approval for new programs has been difficult. State policymakers have also been less willing to provide the resources necessary for research as distinct from teaching. As a result, less selective urban research universities are not satisfied with the quality of their students, the work loads of their faculty, or the status of their institutions within the system of universities serving their state. By contrast, the comprehensive universities have been more concerned with teaching and more interested in developing linkages with their communities. While these institutions have also been concerned about student preparation, they have been less likely to see the solution in terms of more selective admission standards and have been more open to developing strategies for working with those who came.

With few exceptions, moreover, urban universities were created with the expectation that they would serve primarily the residents of the metropolitan area in which they were located. As a result, residence halls were neither planned nor authorized and now are either nonexistent or quite limited in capacity. Coordinating and governing boards have been resistant to permitting the construction of residence halls, partly because of concern about the impact on the residential universities within the system. Three-fourths or more of the students commute from areas contiguous to the universities. As would be expected, urban universities enrolled the highest proportion of minority students in their respective university systems. Where they received criticism from state policymakers, and most did not, it was focused on retention rates rather than on overall minority enrollments. Despite the number of minority students they served, urban universities employed relatively few minority faculty or administrators beyond those who were responsible for special programs that focused on minority students. The exceptions among the universities studied were institutions serving predominantly minority student populations.

Urban universities reflected the stress of accommodating growth during a period of fiscal constraint. Many of the campuses present an unfinished appearance and lack the amenities typically found on a residential campus, such as areas where students can congregate and socialize. Most of the buildings are new, but the absence of maintenance has taken its toll. Walking around an urban campus makes it easy to understand why students often perceive the environment as cold or impersonal.

Many of these universities felt that the public schools in their cities were the worst in the country. This attitude was shared by the news media as well. During the site visits, newspapers in many of the cities routinely carried stories about deficiencies and problems in their school systems. The extent of segregation in residential patterns was reflected in neighborhood schools. Administrators and faculty in several different universities described their respective cities as the most heavily segregated in the country, and each could make a good claim for that dubious distinction. The underprepared students produced by the inner-city schools presented the university with one of its many dilemmas. As one director of admissions pointed out, the entering level competencies required in university programs when contrasted with the underprepared nature of the high school graduates contributed to one major disjuncture between university aspirations and the realities of a commuting student body in an urban setting.

In several cities minority students were said to perceive urban universities as hostile and sometimes racist environments. One black administrator of a special program for minority students summed up the situation when she observed, "Universities treat all students badly, but minority students perceive it as racist." In several of the states, there existed an acknowledged competition between the urban universities and the adjacent urban community colleges for high school graduates. The competition was most intense in those states where the universities exercised very low selectivity and offered extensive remediation to the significant numbers of underprepared students who enrolled. For these universities, attrition was viewed as an escape valve to counter some of the detrimental effects of accepting students without the necessary academic preparation. In general, they did not see themselves as responsible for helping students succeed in the same way that community colleges did.

Universities in the Ford study uniformly emphasized their desire to attract a greater proportion of their enrollment directly from high school in preference to relying to an increasing degree on community college transfers. Yet most of the universities enrolled more than 50 percent of their junior class as transfers. Not all the transfers were from community colleges, but it was common for the community college district serving the same urban area where the university was located to contribute up to one-quarter of the total junior class, or as many as one-half of all transfers. Despite the importance of transfer students to university enrollments, most university recruiting efforts were focused on the high schools.

The attitudes and values of faculty members at universities remain firmly embedded in the traditional academic culture. Research and publication outweigh teaching and service as forms of productivity to which the greatest rewards and recognition are accorded. The choice between employing a qualified faculty member who would make the staff more representative of the student body served and one who would make the department more visible nationally is not a choice at all. Several of the universities in our study were convinced that their heavy teaching loads and less prestigious reputations precluded the recruitment of minority faculty members who could help them in achieving their research objectives.

In these universities, students must adapt to the value preferences and behavioral expectations of the faculty. Those who have problems doing so are not viewed as suitable candidates for a baccalaureate degree. Dropouts and dismissals provide evidence that an institution is maintaining standards, especially in light of the relatively modest admission standards enforced by most urban universities. And special support programs and services have little clout in the competition for scarce institutional resources unless they are funded from external sources. The research university's organizational culture provides little support for nontraditional students in general and for minority students in particular. The latter must look hard to find a friendly black or brown face among those teaching in most of these institutions.

Contrasting the Two Cultures

Table 2 summarizes differences between the cultures of urban community colleges and their university counterparts. The mission of the university emphasizes the generation of knowledge and the development of theory. It is rooted in the basic drive of humanity to probe the mysteries of the universe. The community college mission, by contrast, is community based.

Table 2. A Comparison of Community College and University Cultures.

Cultural Attributes	*Community College*	*University*
Mission emphasis	Community needs	Knowledge generation
Functional priority	Teaching	Research
Assumptions concerning students	Need support system	Independent learners
Concept of quality	Value added (egalitarianism)	Selectivity (elitism)
Curriculum perspective	Remediation/ individualization	Sequencing/specificity
Faculty	Loyalty to institution and discipline	Loyalty to discipline and peer review
Management of academic change	Administrative leadership	Faculty controlled

Programming is derived through the identification of community needs by surveying employers or consulting with service agencies. The distinctiveness of the two cultures grows out of their differences in mission emphasis. Universities are judged on the number of Nobel laureates and merit scholars they have or the number of research projects and publications they sponsor. The "publish or perish" syndrome exemplifies this aspect of the university culture. Community colleges, in contrast, take pride in the teaching function, seeking recognition as the "first" or the "only" institution carrying out a teaching approach or program of study.

A second key difference in cultures can be seen in the assumptions made about students. University faculty expect self-directed, well-prepared, and independent learners. For them, egalitarian goals are met through the admissions process. After this, it is the responsibility of the student to "sink or swim." Community college faculty, by contrast, are receptive to the need for support systems to assist students confronted by academic deficiencies, economic barriers, and limited educational experience in an institution dedicated to access. Most community college administrators and faculty believe they have a responsibility for helping students succeed that goes beyond making academic courses available.

A third difference can be seen in alternative definitions of quality. The university culture emphasizes selectivity and demonstrated achievement when recruiting students or faculty. The test scores and high school ranks of students, as well as the number and source of terminal degrees among the faculty, are matters of considerable importance. Community colleges, however, believe in the concept of "value added" as their measure of quality. Good teaching and appropriate support should be able to overcome deficiencies in student preparation if students are properly motivated. The valued faculty member is one who commands the necessary skills and personality attributes for working with an extremely diverse student population. The source of his or her degree is much less important.

A fourth difference in cultures centers on views of the curriculum. In the university, departmental faculty members emphasize course prerequisites as the basis for a process of knowledge generation that involves both sequential and increasing specialization. This emphasis on vertical components, with introductory courses followed by courses of greater specificity, contrasts with the focus in community colleges on remediation and individualization as the appropriate point of departure for a curriculum in which students must fill gaps, discover career interests, and relate pragmatic objectives to academic disciplines. In the community college, therefore, the college-parallel curriculum tends to be more horizontal and exploratory than vertical and specialized.

The dominant faculty values are also different. University faculty owe their first loyalty to their academic discipline. Their reward structures emphasize this affiliation as well as the recognition that accompanies publication or other achievements sanctioned by a peer-review process administered through national organizations. Community college faculty, while loyal to their academic disciplines, are more oriented toward their local college. Participation in national professional organizations, like publishing and research, is less important for them than for university faculty.

Finally, the management of change is perceived differently. In the university culture, emphasis is given to the responsibility of faculty members for academic programs. The initiation of change occurs through faculty activity at the department level rather than through administrative intervention. But the community college culture relies on faculty loyalty to the institution to provide an environment of acceptance for administratively led change activity.

Those who inhabit these two cultures tend to label differences between them as good or bad, desirable or undesirable. In reality, each culture is a reflection of the differing organizational purposes and societal expectations to which each set of institutions must respond. Articulation problems occur when administrators and faculty members who need to cooperate fail to recognize and respect the differences in the culture of their counterpart institution. Administrators and faculty members in both types of institutions are dedicated to the success of students, but they act out that commitment within their own cultural perspective. Unfortunately, students experience the differences in cultures as incomprehensible barriers to the achievement of their degree objectives.

Conclusion

Two dominant perspectives underlined most of the value differences discussed above. University administrators and faculty saw community colleges as overly protective and prone to condition their students to expectations that were inappropriate for university life. The supportive atmosphere of the community college and its willingness to go to great extremes to facilitate student growth were perceived as injurious to the transfer student who needed to be self-directed and self-disciplined in order to succeed in the university environment. Community college counselors were perceived as indulging students to the point of creating dependency rather than self-initiative. Community college faculty were accused of offering watered-down courses—for example, of using the same textbooks as the universities but not covering the content in scope or depth comparable to that found in university courses.

Community college administrators and faculty were proud of their supportive environment and criticized universities as uncaring or indifferent to the needs of urban students. From their perspective, the attitudes and practices of their university counterparts were deliberately elitist and subversive of the goal of equal access to which community college staff passionately subscribed. Underneath these philosophical differences there was a smoldering resentment among community college faculty and administrators over the condescending attitudes that they saw among university faculty and administrators. They criticized the arrogance of university officials as well as their ignorance of the role of community colleges.

It would be misleading to end this chapter without noting that we have focused on those aspects of institutional culture that contribute the most to forming the barriers urban students encounter in their quest for a baccalaureate degree. In the chapters that follow we try to be more evenhanded in identifying the positive practices that existed or were being tested by many community colleges and universities to improve transfer opportunities. But the conflicting cultures and the barriers they produce fall most heavily on the opportunities experienced by minority students because they are the groups that rely most heavily on community colleges for access. Any effort aimed at reducing the discrepancies between minority and nonminority degree achievement must come to grips with the reality of institutional cultures and their consequences for movement within a state's higher education system.

3

The Urban Community College's Role in Educating Minorities

The community college culture clearly includes a commitment to access and educational opportunity for all students. At the same time, middle-class values dominate the policies, practices, and expectations of their educational programs. In this chapter, we first examine the educational priorities of community colleges and then consider the impact of student service programs. We conclude by discussing the strategies that urban community colleges have identified in their attempts to improve minority student achievement.

Declining enrollments threaten the ability of many urban colleges to offer the range of courses necessary for students to complete associate degree programs within reasonable time periods. The problem affects them in two ways. First, these colleges can make available only a few advanced courses (ones requiring prerequisites) in a sequence that would be acceptable to full-time students. In one college enrolling more than 7,000 students in credit courses, only three sections of advanced mathematics were available during a fall semester. Faculty reported that the college canceled courses needed for academic programs because the large population of underprepared students, along with an emphasis on career programs, left few resources uncommitted. Advanced courses with low enrollments were canceled if they were available elsewhere in the district. The argument that low-enrollment courses required for academic transfer programs need not be offered on every campus was common among the districts visited.

A second problem related to enrollment decline involves the difficulty of supporting high-cost activities such as remedial courses at a level necessary for them to be effective. One college, in recognition of the difficulty of correcting student deficiencies, maintained a ratio of fifteen students to one instructor in developmental courses but was rethinking this commitment because of budget problems. This same college offered a very successful English as a second language program but did not publicize it because enrollment increases in the program were outstripping available resources. The problems of enrollment decline and changing demographics were complicated by the fact that many states were reluctant partners in the higher education remediation enterprise and refused to provide adequate support for this activity.

Educational Priorities and Practices

In many inner-city colleges, transfer programs have not received much emphasis despite the large number of students who express interest in transfer either as an immediate or a long-range objective. At least some of the faculty interviewed suggested that their colleagues had been too quick to accept prevailing judgments about student academic disabilities and had failed to give adequate consideration to student potential. But the emphasis on career programs has also taken its toll. Community college administrators identified reverse transfers from universities as evidence of the lack of utility of baccalaureate-oriented education. At the same time, many faculty members conceded that the surplus of baccalaureate graduates was making community college graduates unemployable in fields such as accounting and computer science, where jobs were once regarded as well within reach of the two-year college graduate. Growing competition from bachelor degree holders may partly explain the increasing number of community college students who indicate an intent to transfer while concurrently pursuing a program designed to lead to immediate employment.

Several urban college districts in our study exhibited little concern about the extent to which courses designated for transfer paralleled the offerings at major receiving institutions. Differences in credit hour arrangements, course sequencing, and prerequisites were justified on the basis of unique mission and the fact that other colleges (most often the ones to which their students rarely transferred) accepted them. Accompanying the lack of concern with parallel course structure was a lack of emphasis on disseminating information about transfer opportunities.

In one college that served a large minority clientele, a small bulletin board in an obscure corner of the counseling center displayed several dated announcements from four-year institutions that were not major receivers of the college's transfers. In more prominent locations around the center and on bulletin boards at the entrance were displayed many attractive materials on career opportunities, job placement, and personal development. The center had program and course guides available for transfers, but it was not clear that these guides would reach students unless they were sufficiently sophisticated to request them or fortunate enough to have an individual interview with a counselor before enrolling, a set of conditions not applying to most minority students at that college.

In another college a large display rack, prominently located in the counseling center, held more than sixty brightly colored brochures, each describing a different occupational program. Among the brochures was one describing a new liberal arts program designed to provide the same assistance to students interested in transferring as the others did for those pursuing career options. This college's district was involved in a debate about whether to permit the development of transfer programs that would emphasize academic majors. Authorizing such programs might have done much to provide a greater sense of balance in institutional emphasis. As it was, this inner-city college was still ahead of many of its counterpart colleges in renewing its emphasis on the liberal arts during a time of declining enrollments and student emphasis on options leading to immediate employment.

Standards. The trend in the late seventies and early eighties has been to neglect transfer programs in favor of unique functions not shared with four-year colleges. A correlate practice—permitting students without the necessary reading and writing skills to enroll in college-parallel courses—has produced distrust about the quality and standards of community college courses among four-year institutions. Community college faculty admitted candidly that the rigor of the courses they taught did not match that expected in the four-year setting. A chemistry professor observed:

> Let's be truthful. I've gotten used to the idea that we use comparable textbooks, but we cover fewer chapters and we give less rigorous tests. We're not communicating as much information.

Interestingly, the problem did not extend across the board. In allied health programs, selective admissions ensured a better prepared student body. A dean of one such program noted that course standards in his area were the same as they were anywhere else.

Perceptions of differences in rigor extend to other organizations within the communities served by inner-city community colleges. One community college had for nearly twenty years provided under contract the general education courses taken by students at two nearby hospital schools of nursing. Recently, this responsibility was assumed by the university to which most of the students from the community college transferred. The argument advanced successfully by the university in displacing the community college was that its courses could better prepare nursing students who wanted to earn the baccalaureate degree.

There appeared to be wide diversity in the standards applied for successful completion of the same course on different campuses of the same district. At one extreme, a major receiving university reported no measurable differences in writing and math competencies between students who graduated from an adjacent community college and those who entered the university directly from the inner-city high schools that fed both the community college and the university. This phenomenon could not be attributed to high admission standards at the university since it, like the community college, served a student population that by any measure would be described as seriously underprepared. Interestingly, in the area of reading skills, where the community college required students to correct deficiencies, the university reported satisfactory preparation. In this instance, the use of an assessment exam accompanied by mandatory placement and the assessment of exit competencies clearly produced better preparation in reading among students who remained underprepared in skills where these practices were not enforced.

A different college in the same district, attended by a much less heavily minority student population, was frequently mentioned by receiving universities as producing highly qualified transfer students who were capable of holding their own with native university students in advanced level courses. Such wide differences in student preparation influenced university recruiting practices, as well as the evaluation of transcripts. One of two receiving universities had avoided entering into articulation agreements so that differences in transfer students' prior preparation could be taken into account in the transcript evaluation process.

Tolerance of different standards for the same courses in different colleges of the same district was made easier by the absence of systematic follow-up information. Districts had only fragmentary information on the performance of transfer students, and such data were rarely collected routinely, even though districts were aware of the potential problems caused by the lack of such information. Problems arising from varying standards were partly exacerbated and partly glossed over by the use of norm-referenced grading standards that placed substantial emphasis on effort and progress rather than on any defined set of expected exit competencies.

Liberal withdrawal policies also played a role. Such policies in combination with norm-referenced grading typically produced high grade point averages, which in turn contributed to disparities between the grades earned by students before and after transferring. Such disparities were noticeably greater for transfer students from inner-city colleges than for their more suburban counterparts. In one urban college, 80 percent of the grades awarded for the semester preceding this study were *A*'s and *B*'s or *W*'s. Not surprisingly, many district administrators steadfastly denied that the colleges under their supervision observed different standards. But they did so as an act of faith and not on the basis of objective evidence.

Administrators, in fact, seemed largely unaware of problems involving course standards. In one urban community college, the president, concerned with the high failure rate in an accounting course, gave his faculty two choices. They could either develop an open-entry, open-exit approach to teaching the course, which would allow students to begin wherever they were and take whatever time was needed to succeed in the course, or they could develop a new course taught the traditional way in which most students would succeed. The faculty chose the latter course and worked out a course in technical accounting. Success rates are now satisfactory to the president.

This example illustrates an assumption commonly held by community college administrators. If students do not pass courses in sufficiently large numbers, the problem must rest with the instructional methodology or the attitudes of the faculty. Accepting the idea that a majority of the students attending a college were unprepared to do much, if not most, of the work offered and could not be brought up to acceptable standards through innovative teaching methods and instructor diligence seemed to strike at the core of the philosophical concepts that undergird the open-door community college. So the easiest approach by far was to tailor courses to student capabilities. The deception was supported by the absence of evaluative information on student performance other than grades based on institutional norms.

Despite much evidence that institutional resources are

concentrated in career program areas, many senior administrators insisted that equal emphasis was being given to transfer programs. In some respects their argument was a reasonable one. Faculty salaries represent the single largest area of institutional expenditures, and most full-time faculty, hired in the early periods of institutional growth, taught academic rather than career-related courses. Even though the weight of evidence suggested that transfer programs had been neglected in the past, there were efforts in most districts to establish a better balance between serving the underprepared and recruiting the well qualified. Also observed was an effort to achieve better balance between career and transfer offerings.

Program Emphasis as a Function of Race. On one level there is much to be said for concentrating vocational/technical offerings on those campuses where students are the least well prepared to undertake baccalaureate-oriented work. The problem arises when the campuses offering high concentrations of occupational programs turn out always to be located in areas serving high concentrations of minority students. Community college districts serving large urban areas have some of the most uneven racial distributions to be found in any sector of public education anywhere in the country. While districts are sometimes unjustly accused of having located campuses to achieve segregation, the enrollment demographics not infrequently support this criticism. Districts may include one or more campuses that are predominantly or almost exclusively made up of minority students; ten or fifteen miles away, a second campus may enroll a student body that is less than 5 percent minority. While segregated campuses can be rationalized in terms of the development of urban districts, the situation becomes more problematic when racial imbalance is accompanied by educational programs that track minority students disproportionately into lower-status occupations. Concentrating occupational offerings on campuses serving the highest proportions of minorities while concurrently permitting transfer programs to decline in availability and quality approaches dangerously close to becoming a self-fulfilling prophecy. In other words, minorities become vocational/technical majors because no viable alternatives are provided to them.

While urban community college districts were vulnerable to criticism on the basis of the racial imbalances among their campuses, they deserve considerable credit for the progress that they have made in achieving racially balanced staffs both at the college and district level. Administrators have placed high priority on recruiting minority administrators and faculty members and have achieved observable results. Indeed, several of the districts were led at the highest levels by minority administrators who, as a rule, appeared more concerned about standards and the erosion of transfer programs than did their nonminority counterparts. The situation was not, however, uniformly positive. In some of the older colleges, particularly in those experiencing enrollment declines, the proportion of minority faculty lagged far behind a changing student population. In one such college a white president observed:

> The absence of minority faculty members is not a problem here. A good faculty member can deal with any student as long as he is not biased.

For the most part, however, minority students have a much better chance of finding role models in community colleges than in the institutions to which they ultimately transfer.

General Study Degree. Contributing to the image problems of community colleges is the tendency for most districts to offer a general studies degree. This program, while known by various names, has as its distinguishing characteristic that it does not require students to take courses for which other courses are a prerequisite. The program is also characterized by extreme flexibility in its required distribution so that it fits almost any combination of courses that a student might conceivably take. Faculty described this as a "garbage program" because it was used more as a tool for keeping students eligible for student aid and for padding graduation statistics than as a means of defining objectives toward which students might work. One faculty member described the general studies program at his institution in this way:

> There are no clear goals, and it is analogous to a bus full of passengers who have quite different destinations in mind, with few actually aware of the final destination or the value of that destination in their own life.

Because of their character, general studies programs became the dumping ground for undecided students, for late registrants, and for students with weak academic backgrounds. Students from general studies programs may subsequently seek transfer credit despite statements by the college that the general studies program was not designed for students interested in earning a bachelor's degree. When this occurs, the credibility of community college academic programs with university faculty can be seriously impaired.

Academic Support Services. A study by Richardson, Fisk, and Okun (1983) earlier reported a decline in student reading and writing of connected prose in one urban community college. In place of text-oriented reading or writing, researchers found students learning bits of information by scanning instructor handouts or copying notes from instructors' lectures. Students were then tested for recognition of information bits on multiple-choice examinations. This fragmented learning process (sometimes called *bitting*) concerned researchers because it seemed to foster dependence on the instructor rather than to encourage student independence in the learning process.

Critics of the study have questioned the extent to which a declining emphasis on critical literacy observed in one college is characteristic of community colleges in general. However, comments made by academic support staff in the community colleges in our study suggested that the problem was widespread. Thus, several librarians were critical of faculty and administration for not recognizing the key role that the library plays in a baccalaureate program. They noted that the university expects students to be prepared to do library research while community college faculty seldom called for much more than a book report or supplemental reading in their courses. Public libraries in the neighborhoods in which low-income students reside were described as typically quite limited in comparison with those in suburban neighborhoods. The same deficiency confronted the low-income students in their public school libraries. One librarian observed:

> During our orientation days, students are brought on tour to the library. When I ask them if they know how to use a library and if they have used the library in the past, they will always answer in the affirmative. They don't want to be embarrassed by what they don't know, a fact which becomes apparent as I unobtrusively probe their level of understanding during the hour they are here. Yet, I cannot convince my college that we should have a one- or two-hour course on library use.

Another librarian observed:

> This college has gotten away from the concept that the heart of the institution is the library because it is a commuter institution. Our students don't utilize or congregate around the library as they do at residential institutions.

At a college where the library was known as the learning resource center, discussion of the nontraditional student as a learner provoked the following observation:

> Our minority students are visually literate, even when they are poor readers. They tend to learn better from the use of nonprint media in classrooms than from books and other print media. Our faculty utilize this reality without considering the

> consequences on reading development. We are experiencing growing use of nonprint media by our faculty and a decline in assigned library work.

The state in which this institution is located has prescribed a minimum number of words that must be written by all students in public colleges and universities during their freshman and sophomore years. The director of the learning resource center observed that more and more faculty were using films and related audiovisual aids as the basis for student writing in compliance with the state requirement rather than having students write as a result of assigned readings. He observed that "our humanities faculty are the highest users of nonprint media, with science and the applied arts next in line."

Another librarian was critical of the testing policies and procedures at her college as faculty increasingly used multiple-choice tests, including tests selected from computer banks of test items. She declared:

> Our Hispanic minority is particularly prone to memorize. I don't know whether it is a cultural pattern or the product of their schooling. But they tend not to organize their thinking in any kind of synthesis, nor do they analytically question what they have been learning. Yet, our testing policies reinforce that rote memorization.

In addition to libraries or learning resource centers, most community colleges provided special laboratories and tutorial assistance to students who were underprepared in the basic skills. Administrators favored technological applications such as computer-assisted instruction (the University of Illinois PLATO System was used extensively in several colleges) over labor-intensive solutions such as tutoring. However, minority students were described by faculty who worked closely with them as resistant to self-paced, automated, drop-in laboratories. Thus, it was not uncommon to pass nearly empty automated learning laboratories on the same campus where there was a waiting list for tutorial assistance.

Minority students were said to respond best to a structured learning environment in which role models provided support and encouragement. Despite this assessment, the use of learning laboratories on most campuses was voluntary, and record keeping and follow-up procedures were not designed to maintain continuing contact with a student. The two institutions that did have highly structured monitoring and follow-up procedures supported by computer processing had the strongest and best designed procedures for identifying academic problems. They also offered well-designed and well-balanced intervention strategies for helping students overcome their learning problems.

Student Services

Student services components have provided much of the leadership in efforts to adapt the community college environment to the needs of disadvantaged and underprepared students. This approach has both its good and bad features. On the positive side, the most significant affirmative action gains have occurred among student service staff members. Partly for this reason, minority counselors and other student support service workers have come to see themselves as special advocates for the disadvantaged and the underprepared. Their commitment to these students has done much to promote the nurturing environment that is often cited as a major strength of the community college in working with high-risk groups. On the negative side, the existence of a special cadre of staff who see themselves as protectors of the open-door philosophy for the underprepared has produced fewer academic solutions than desirable, since merely keeping underprepared students enrolled and qualified for financial assistance cannot be an end in itself. At best, the rift between academic and student services staffs slows needed change and contributes to dysfunctions in student advising. At worst, it can erupt into conflicts that stymie efforts to deal with the issues of academic quality and standards.

In one district, academic administrators came to the conclusion that if transfer institutions did not accept *D* grades, perhaps the community college should also change its policy. After considerable study and discussion with faculty, a new policy was formulated that would have had the effect of tightening standards. But the proposal was stalemated when the student personnel administrators' organization within the district adopted the position that the policy was detrimental to the philosophy of the college and the needs of the minorities it served.

Other common areas for controversy between academic and student support staffs included the appropriate use of entrance exams, whether course placement should be advisory or mandatory, and the degree of rigor to be applied in enforcing standards for student progress. It is an oversimplification to present these issues as defining the boundaries between student services and instruction. Nevertheless, the differences were observed more frequently than not. In the following discussion of student services, we have emphasized practices that affect opportunities for minority students to achieve the baccalaureate degree.

Admissions. Urban community colleges, without exception, welcomed all who sought admission. High school graduates, adults with general equivalency diplomas (GED), and those who were eighteen years of age or older were all admissible. Some high school-age students were even allowed to enroll if they had the consent of their school districts. Interestingly, those with the GED outperformed high school graduates in several cities. Not surprisingly, those without the GED or a high school diploma were extremely unlikely to carry their community college studies through to completion.

Admission to these colleges did not include the right to enroll in any program offered. High-cost programs and those requiring certification examinations were typically quite selective. Many students spent as long as two years completing general education prerequisites and making up deficiencies before being admitted to selective programs. Competition for the limited number of seats available was stiffened by reverse transfers from four-year institutions who applied for admission to programs such as dental hygiene and nursing after having completed up to a baccalaureate degree program elsewhere. Typically, minority students were underrepresented in these selective programs. The use of relatively rigorous admission standards in high-cost, high-demand programs, while preserving and defending the student's right to enter lower-cost college transfer programs without regard to previous preparation, reveals one of the major unsolved paradoxes of the community college philosophy.

Recruiting. Many faculty members and administrators believe that the emphasis urban community colleges place on employment as the primary reason for going to college has undermined the transfer function. Urban community colleges typically are institutions of last resort for most of their students. The existence of this "captive clientele" was reflected in recruiting practices that tended to be traditional and conservative, except for sporadic advertising campaigns when enrollment declines threatened college budgets. Most of the burden fell on admissions staff members who performed obligatory visits to high school counselors who, in turn, worked diligently to get their best prepared students into the more prestigious institutions. Sometimes the efforts of admissions counselors were augmented by faculty members who wanted to preserve their jobs or their programs or who had been given release time from other responsibilities.

One college used a "credit in escrow" program to encourage current high school students to enroll in college-level courses, and two others had advanced registration policies to allow high school seniors to register for college-level courses prior to graduation. Increasingly, urban campuses offered tuition scholarships to emphasize their interest in academically able students and to try to change their image as institutions serving primarily a remedial population. But despite their best efforts, inner-city colleges were captives of the extreme underpreparation of their enrollees. The differences between students attending inner-city colleges and their more suburban counterparts were nowhere better reflected than in the experiences of one district in which 100 scholarships were made available to each of its colleges. All available scholarships were used by a more suburban college while the inner-city school had difficulty in awarding three.

Some districts have used extensive advertising on radio stations or in newspapers that target blacks or Hispanics. In one district where these approaches were in use, a minority division chairman nonetheless observed:

> Community colleges don't really know how to recruit minorities. People no longer accept figures on how many; it makes a difference why you recruit. People want to know what is being done for those who attend.

Despite high minority enrollments in community colleges, the chairman had a point. During the course of the study it became clear that minority students attended the most prestigious institutions to which they could gain admittance with a single-mindedness exceeding that of their nonminority counterparts. Community colleges did enroll large numbers of minority students, but assessment figures, where available, suggested that very few of them were qualified to do college work by traditional academic standards. Inner-city community colleges, in the minds of those who led them and those who taught in them, were frequently places that offered very limited opportunities for the academically prepared. Not surprisingly, prospective students shared this perception.

Assessment and Placement. Most community colleges have well-developed assessment procedures for placing students in English and math courses. Many also assess students' reading levels, and some require a writing sample. Remedial courses are prescribed when deficiencies are identified. Clearly, the trend is in the direction of greater rigor in assessment and less flexibility in course placement for students who lack prerequisite skills. There has been much talk of entrance and exit competencies, but few colleges have actually developed competency-based transfer programs.

Underlying discussions of greater rigor in assessment was a pervasive concern about enrollment declines and the impact that more rigorous assessment and progress standards might have on this phenomenon. In discussions with faculty in one district, those from the popular areas of business and computer science were vociferous in their support for keeping underprepared students out of regular classes. Their colleagues in the social sciences and humanities were strangely silent. When asked directly if underprepared students who lacked reading and writing competencies were a problem in social science and humanities classes, faculty members from these areas squirmed a little and then said, "No." In later discussions in this district and elsewhere, it became clear that faculty members in fields with small enrollments, such as the humanities, were reluctant to support rigorous assessment and placement because they were concerned that the resulting loss of enrollments would threaten their opportunity to teach extra courses for extra pay, if not their job security.

Assessment procedures and the rigor with which they were enforced varied as much within some districts as they did across districts. Some colleges assessed most or all of their entering students through math, English, and reading tests, which were supplemented by a writing sample. In such colleges, placement procedures tended to be mandatory, subject to the right of appeal. Interestingly, colleges with more rigorous testing and placement procedures did not seem to suffer in terms of enrollment, despite the often expressed concern of many faculty members and administrators that enrollment problems would inevitably occur if greater rigor were to be introduced. Colleges with more rigorous procedures tended to be those with better reputations for academic quality, and they thus were the ones to which students migrated in search of educational opportunities.

This phenomenon does not bode well for inner-city campuses serving high concentrations of minority students. Most of their students make decisions about attending college too late for effective assessment and placement. In our study, administrators with one eye on their budgets were reluctant to approve procedures that might discourage potential students even when they were sympathetic to the need for better assessment and placement.

Once assessed, students typically found themselves in one

of three beginning levels of English. Again, the standards for initial placement differed within districts, as well as across districts, as a function of the general level of student preparation. At one extreme, students were placed in the most elementary sequence if they read below the fifth-grade level. On a different campus in the same district but with a better prepared entering class, the comparable standard was seventh-grade reading ability. In this district about 40 percent of the students in the inner-city institution were placed in the lowest tier. By contrast, the sister college reported placing only 20 percent of its students in the lowest tier, even though it set higher standards. The differences were equally dramatic for placement in the second tier. The inner-city college reported that 50 percent of its students were placed in this tier based on a ninth-grade cutoff point. Using a tenth-grade standard, the sister institution reported that only 30 percent of its students were in the lower tier.

Many faculty members believe that reading ability is a poor predictor of writing skills. By preference, they used writing samples whenever circumstances permitted. The procedures used in one college that assessed 97 percent of its entering classes were typical. Essays were initially read by two faculty members; if they disagreed on placement, the essay was read by a third person. Care was taken to ensure that those reading the essays remained unaware of the student's gender, age, or race. Without exception, appeal procedures were available for students who believed that they had been misplaced. Students had the opportunity to talk with faculty members, a division chair, a counselor, and/or a dean. A student who did not utilize the appeal process still could be identified and moved to a different class by an alert instructor. Not surprisingly, faculty members reported satisfaction with placement procedures, especially when writing samples were used.

Assessment procedures in mathematics most commonly relied on instructor-developed tests. Because inner-city students are not well prepared, they avoid math courses whenever possible. Partly for this reason, fewer than half of the entering students were assessed in math in many urban colleges. The tendency of students to avoid math may be unintentionally abetted by these institutions through a reluctance to require math in degree programs or through assessment procedures that permit students to enroll in almost all courses except English and math without assessment. One district, for example, permitted students to earn an associate of arts degree (its basic transfer credential) without completing any courses in math, even though the bachelor's degrees in institutions to which students regularly transferred could not be completed without demonstrating competency in mathematics.

Financial Aid. This kind of assistance is essential for most minority students who attend urban colleges. Given the statistics on unemployment and poverty among minority youth, it is not surprising that the percentage of students receiving financial aid closely parallels the proportion of minority students in attendance. Among colleges serving inner-city populations, the number on financial aid may be as high as 85 percent. The time between admission and actual receipt of financial aid, particularly from federal programs, often is the most difficult period for urban students. Some are unable to pay the costs of required textbooks, others find it difficult even to pay for transportation. In response, many urban colleges have established special policies and practices to assist poor students. It was common for colleges to provide tuition waivers to those who had applied for financial assistance and who appeared to qualify for it but had not yet received funds. Less common, but available in several colleges, were bookstore vouchers to permit purchase of textbooks and necessary academic supplies before the arrival of assistance checks. Instructors were also encouraged to avoid giving assignments in required texts until arrangements had been made for students to obtain them. While small, these adjustments were often critical to successful matriculation for the most severely disadvantaged.

Unfortunately, however, some community college practices designed to help disadvantaged students may ultimately produce undesirable side effects. Permitting students to repeat courses where an initial effort resulted in a low or failing grade keeps them eligible for financial aid and provides the time many require to overcome academic deficiencies. Students experience problems, however, when they transfer after using three of their five years of eligibility for financial aid while having earned only a year or less of credits applicable to a baccalaureate degree. Institutional policies seem deliberately ambivalent about appropriate objectives for the student who is more than mildly remedial at the time of entry to a community college.

The federal regulations for student progress and eligibility for financial assistance implemented in January 1984 may do much to resolve this ambivalence. Prior to establishment of these regulations, many community colleges permitted withdrawal from courses without penalty through the fifteenth week of a sixteen-week semester. Under the new regulations, students have to complete, with a passing grade, at least 75 percent of the courses that they attempt if they are to remain eligible for aid. The regulations for student progress are only the most recent of a series of changing requirements for veterans' benefits and federal financial aid perceived by the colleges to have adversely affected more than one-fourth of their students. In one inner-city college, counselors reported a decline in the proportion of students eligible for financial assistance from 77 to 41 percent over a five-year period.

Apart from their obvious impact on enrollments, staff members were not certain whether the new regulations were detrimental to student and institutional interests. One observed:

> Students used to come in and pick up their checks and go out with no one concerned about whether they were pursuing a particular program or just returning to the streets. Now all that has changed.

The transportability of federal assistance was not an issue in any of the colleges in our study. Financial aid officers described relationships with four-year institutions as cordial and effective. For state-administered financial assistance, however, the picture was less favorable. Legislatures in several states provided less than full funding to state plans. In some states, the priority was clearly on reducing differences between the costs of attending public and independent institutions rather than on increasing access for low-income students. Problems arose primarily when midyear transfers did not receive the increase in assistance to which their attendance at a higher-cost institution entitled them.

Strategies for Promoting Student Achievement

The problems presented by urban students have evoked a wide range of interventions among inner-city colleges. The interventions run the gamut from motivational activities to tightening academic standards. Assessment and the use of exit competencies were under study or in the beginning stages of implementation in most urban districts. Some of the strategies that have assumed increasing importance as urban districts work to improve opportunities for student success are described in the following section.

Motivational Strategies. Community colleges that had minority leaders and served predominantly minority populations often placed emphasis on motivational activities. One college described its graduation exercises as an honors convocation. In addition to awarding degrees and certificates, the college honored all students who achieved a *B* average for the preceding semester, regardless of their previous work. The honors convocation, a major social activity for the college, was well attended by the students and the larger community.

Another district operated two major programs named for nationally prominent black leaders who had grown up in the community. Some districts treated all students who had earned a specified number of credits with a minimum grade point average as potential transfers or potential graduates. Such students were sent letters congratulating them on their progress and providing them with information about how they could capitalize on their achievements. One college reported that it had doubled the number of students graduating through this approach, and another college reported a significant increase in the number of students who transferred. While these and other motivational approaches might appear cosmetic from an external perspective, their frequent use in urban institutions with predominantly minority populations and the effects reported for them suggest that they have considerable potential for improving achievement among minority students. The motivational strategies have in common the attempt to raise people's aspirations, and this function may be critical for inner-city youth.

Affirmative action was also viewed as providing motivation for minority students to succeed. In one district, the chancellor noted that the knowledge barriers between community colleges and the university were less important than attitudinal barriers. Students' aspirations, their socialization patterns, their survival orientation, and their unwillingness to defer short-term gratification inhibit opportunities for success. By recruiting minority faculty and emphasizing motivation, this district tried to promote the college as a place for discovery of individual talents rather than as a supermarket where customers accumulated credits toward a degree. In support of this concept, the chancellor believed that it was extremely important for inner-city colleges to emphasize athletic programs, social programs, and the cultural arts as well as academic work.

Finally, orientation programs are making a comeback. Many colleges are devoting serious efforts to assist students with program planning rather than simply enrolling them in discrete courses, as had come to be the norm in the growth-oriented seventies. Better information about program opportunities early in a student's college career not only improves his or her motivation but in addition reduces the probability that he or she will lose credits when transferring.

Academic Strategies. A variety of such strategies have been tried in community colleges. Team-taught interdisciplinary courses have been around for years, but they are receiving renewed attention as a means of providing more coherence to a learning environment fragmented by the growing number of part-time students and faculty. In our visits it was common to find reading instruction offered on an individual basis and in conjunction with courses in composition. One college offered supplemental reading instruction to students in a political science course. Students were tested after the first week of classes, and those judged deficient were given the option of enrolling in a one-credit course in reading that used materials relevant to the political science course. Another college required a foreign language in a newly adopted liberal arts option. Faculty members candidly admitted that one of the important reasons for doing so was to improve the credibility of the college as a place where serious students could find an appropriate challenge.

Several colleges provided special transition courses for students moving from remedial to regular college work. For students in these transition courses, the number of contact hours was increased, allowing them more time to work with the instructor to master the content. Sometimes reading and composition were taught as part of the same course, but this approach presumed teacher preparation that was not always available. Several urban colleges had developed transition courses in both the physical and the social sciences. In some settings, the developmental instructor and the regular course instructor worked as a team, conferring on content and coordinating the sequence of topics covered.

One of the issues confronted by those who work with underprepared students is finding enough credit hours of work to keep them qualified for financial aid without placing them in courses requiring the basic skills that they are currently enrolled in remedial courses to learn. In one college, staff in each career program area had been encouraged to develop at least one course applicable to an associate degree that could be completed successfully with minimal reading and writing skills. In another institution, teachers of remedial courses worked with their colleagues in other disciplines to develop supplemental reading materials that were consistent with the vocabulary level of remedial students. Increasingly, limits have been set on the time students are given to correct deficiencies. Those colleges that have studied success rates of remedial students (most of the colleges have not) have generally found that students who subsequently succeed in regular programs complete their remedial work in one or, at most, two semesters. The prognosis for any student who requires more time is very dim; this is true, at least in part, because state and federal financial aid regulations are geared to provide only this period of eligibility.

Identifying the competencies that a course is designed to provide is not a new experience for community colleges. Faculty members in nursing programs have long required assessment of entering and exit competencies to make certain that graduates can pass state licensing examinations. Nursing faculty have been so successful using this approach that graduates of community college programs in many states now outperform the graduates of baccalaureate institutions on the same state examination. One district applied the experience gained with nursing classes to all vocational offerings. Course competencies were then aggregated into program competencies, and prospective employers were given a description of the range of tasks that a program graduate was qualified to perform.

Developing entrance and exit competencies has proven more controversial for transfer offerings than for vocational programs. One district that had used an examination to measure exit competencies for graduates of college-parallel programs during the early sixties subsequently dropped it during the movement toward mass access. Replacing the exam were syllabi that faculty signed to indicate that their procedures for instruction and evaluation were designed to ensure that students accomplished stated and measurable objectives. But there was no external check on outcomes. Because of the extreme disparities among students completing the same courses in different colleges of this district, consideration was being given to reinstating the exam or finding a suitable alternative to it.

While testing for exit competencies in transfer courses was a practice in only one of the colleges participating in the study, the possibility of such tests was under consideration by faculty committees in several additional districts. One of the factors influencing discussions was the growing tendency for four-year colleges and universities to administer their own validation examinations or, alternatively, to hold credit in escrow until a transfer student completed the next course in a particular sequence. In effect, community college administrators are beginning to see the handwriting on the wall. If community colleges do not test for exit competencies, their students will be tested by the upper-division institutions to which they transfer. On the horizon for several states was the so-called rising junior examination already required in Florida and Georgia. Such exams require students to demonstrate proficiency on a standardized scale before they are permitted to matriculate as juniors.

The impetus for improved assessment of entry and exit competencies was by no means a function of external pressures or influences from the faculty alone. The dean of one urban college noted, "If you let people walk in off the street and enroll in class, you are hopelessly lost because you give teachers an insurmountable task." When confronted with such a task, faculty members must choose between reducing standards or increasing attrition rates. Neither of these alternatives is acceptable, and so the search continues for strategies that offer some chance of improving student success without violating the community college commitment to open access.

Standards for student progress help to tie together the academic strategies. Colleges increasingly give attention to finding out whether students are making satisfactory progress. As previously noted, federal financial regulations have given major impetus to this movement. Still, the policies of most districts remained fairly minimal. A typical district required a minimum grade point average of 1.5 (on a 4-point scale) by the time that a student had completed twelve credit hours, while concurrently moving the date for withdrawal from a course without penalty from the end of the fourteenth week of the semester to the end of the tenth week. Course completion requirements were those required by federal policy.

Complicating efforts to enforce standards of progress was the nearly uniform absence of effective student tracking systems. Despite these handicaps, however, there has been some progress. Several districts required periodic academic audits of students who were receiving financial aid. Overall there was recognition of the need for better student guidance and more rigorous academic standards. One black president summed up the needed action very well: "Professionally, we must map the paths and give no quarter in terms of the standards we require; we must be very clear about expected outcomes."

Academic Support Strategies. Community colleges placed considerable emphasis on academic support services. The learning laboratory was the most emphasized intervention. Within learning laboratories can be found most of the support services that have proven themselves over the past decade. These laboratories perform initial diagnoses of student deficiencies and prescribe learning modules or tutorial services as required. They administer mastery exams and preserve records of student progress. Many labs are assigned to faculty who provide special assistance and individual attention.

Within the learning labs, heavy emphasis was frequently placed on technological solutions to learning problems. In particular, use of such computer-assisted instructional programs as PLATO has been very popular. Almost without exception, this material is of high quality and demonstrated effectiveness. As noted earlier, technological solutions are favored by administrators over such labor-intensive interventions as tutorial services and individualized faculty assistance because the former are seen as more efficient. Technological solutions, for example, have the important advantage of being always available. Unfortunately, the experience of inner-city colleges seems to show that underprepared students prefer human interventions because of their need for both support and role models. Technological solutions require self-motivated and self-directed learners, a description that does not apply to most students attending inner-city institutions.

The faculty favored separate learning labs offered by the departments having responsibility for remediation over the centralized learning labs preferred by administrators. While not as efficient in terms of space and personnel as the centralized learning laboratory, discipline-related laboratories have the advantage of emphasizing the relationship between the exercises provided and the skills necessary to succeed in advanced courses offered by the same department.

Regardless of whether learning laboratories were centralized or discipline affiliated, the most important service they provided was tutoring by professionals, paraprofessionals, or peers. Peer tutors proved most successful in those colleges that provided professionals who trained, organized, and evaluated them. In some institutions tutors were assigned directly to classes to ensure they came into regular contact with prospective clients. Attending class had the additional advantage of familiarizing tutors with course content and instructor expectations. Alternatively, tutors were assigned to a centralized learning laboratory where they served students on a walk-in basis. Among the advantages cited for this arrangement were ease of administration and use of time in tutoring that would otherwise have been spent in attending class. The greatest disadvantage involved the difficulty of getting students most in need of tutorial services to take advantage of them. With educational as well as social services, those who need them the least are most likely to take advantage of them. One college dealt with this problem by sending out letters to students in high-risk groups encouraging the use of tutorial services and implying that eligibility for financial aid might be threatened if the student did not use the services. As might be expected, faculty preferred to have tutors assigned directly to a class.

One college that limited tutorial services did so in part because the source of funding was a small categorical state grant that limited participants to those who were both vocationally oriented and disadvantaged. This state policy clearly emphasized vocational education at the expense of the transfer program. When asked why the college did not use its own resources to make tutorial services more widely available, the answer of the person responsible for the services was, "Students don't request such services." When it was observed that a sister college in the same district that attracted more capable students made heavy use of tutorial services, the instructor suggested that the difference should be attributed to the socioeconomic background of the students. This particular combination of state influence and staff attitude seemed to suggest a limited view of the capabilities of the student population served, a theme that recurred regularly in discussions with the staffs of inner-city colleges.

Conclusion

The contents of this chapter will provide few surprises to those who are familiar with urban community colleges. Such institutions serve students who are disadvantaged educationally and economically. The task they have taken on is monumental but they persist. And, slowly, the problem has begun to yield to the combination of human and technological interventions that these colleges employ. Progress has been modest and setbacks have been frequent. Still, the high level of commitment of urban community colleges to the clientele they serve, along with their willingness to commit institutional resources to special support programs when state categorical grants are reduced or foundation funds expire, make them critical actors in any attempt to reduce discrepancies between the educational achievement of minorities and that of nonminorities.

Urban community colleges can be criticized for compromising standards, emphasizing a social welfare rather than an educational mission, overemphasizing technological solutions, and coming perilously close to confirming the criticisms of those who allege that they constitute a class-based tracking system. But they must be commended for their belief in the basic dignity of all human beings, their increasing sophistication in diagnosing and dealing with a broad array of learning problems, their willingness to put their resources where their philosophy takes them, and their success in recruiting a large percentage of all the minority faculty members and administrators currently involved in American higher education.

Beyond these obvious contributions to helping minority students succeed, there are hopeful signs on the horizon that point to future progress, albeit of an evolutionary nature. Among the most promising signs is the tendency of urban community colleges to rely more on institutional research in revising policy and less on philosophy. As an example, one college studied the outcomes for three groups in determining whether to make course placement mandatory on the basis of reading test scores. One group was left to do as it pleased, a second enrolled in existing developmental courses, and a third was required to enroll in a program especially tailored to its assessed competencies. All members of the first group were gone by the end of the first semester. The second group did better, but not nearly so well as the third. This college now assesses all entering students and mandates placement on the basis of the results.

In another study conducted in the same college, information gathered on a math course with an extremely high failure rate indicated that those students who entered the course from a prerequisite remedial course experienced problems but that those who entered by way of the placement exam performed well. When this information was made available to the math department, the problem was soon resolved. Besides using institutional research to identify and resolve problems of student learning, community colleges seem to be increasingly aware of the need to improve the available data base and to rely more heavily on information in decision making. This use of an improved information base in decision making holds the hope of a better understanding of the issues that currently separate community colleges and universities in their efforts to provide effective educational services to an urban clientele.

4

Effecting the Transition to Urban Universities

A majority of the universities participating in this study could be characterized as emerging or established research universities. They value scholarship over teaching or service. While these institutions were originally established to serve residents of their urban settings, the aspirations of their administrators and faculty lead naturally to priorities focused on national recognition and improved status within their respective state university systems. The conflicting demands of urban settings and national aspirations produce dynamic tension that inhibits wholehearted pursuit of either set of objectives. Beyond the conflicting demands of setting and aspirations, there are additional complications arising from system constraints and pressures from state political leadership.

An institution that pursues research status in the midst of a city experiencing a wide array of social problems faces difficult decisions. Making choices between teaching-oriented minority candidates willing to devote time to serving as role models for minority students and nonminority candidates with stronger research qualifications exemplifies the problem that continues through the tenure decision and beyond. Complicating this choice process is the widely held perception that emerging urban universities are not competitive in recruiting qualified minority scholars because they have heavier teaching loads than do more established research universities. Despite conflicting objectives and difficult choices, however, urban universities perform their missions at levels that generally exceed public expectations. They enroll a higher proportion of minority students than any other institutions in their systems, and, even though most have few minorities on their administrative staffs or faculty, many employ intervention strategies of demonstrated effectiveness to help minority students succeed.

In this chapter, we expand our previous discussion on urban university culture to examine in detail practices related to educational program and support services. In the course of this analysis, we highlight some of the disjunctures between university practices and those within community colleges where most educationally disadvantaged minority students begin their postsecondary educational careers.

Educational Priorities and Practices

Many urban universities are products of the expansion of educational opportunities that occurred in the 1960s. Even those that predated this era underwent significant change; for example, they may have moved from two-year to four-year status, changed from independent to public institutions, or simply increased significantly in stature. In one case, a school became a university by public referendum. But their master plans, conceived in the heady environment of higher education's "golden era," often projected more students, more buildings, and more educational programs, particularly at the graduate level, than most have been able to achieve. Shifting demographics and fiscal realities played undeniable roles in the frustration of their ambitions, but also important have been the competition and political influence of less urban sister institutions, which often have done all in their power to prevent urban universities from developing programs that might siphon off their students.

As one result, most urban universities believe they need to offer additional degree programs at both the graduate and undergraduate levels. This is as true of the comprehensive institutions as of the research universities. And it seems to apply to universities that have followed relatively normal development patterns as well as those in which program development has been curtailed by fiscal constraints and/or competition within their systems. There are also the normal problems of faculty imbalance. Colleges of arts and sciences and of education have fewer students and more faculty than they need while the opposite applies to such professional areas as business and engineering. Available resources and student demand have significantly impacted admission standards and retention practices among many of the colleges that comprise each university.

The problem of improving baccalaureate achievement by minorities appears to be primarily a problem of retention. Given the limited remedial offerings and support staff available for underprepared students already enrolled in urban universities, it was difficult to see how the admission of additional underprepared students would improve the situation. While none of the universities were turning away qualified minority students, the retention of students was not a priority for most of them. In one, the chair of the faculty retention committee indicated that she had not called the committee together in more than a year because there seemed to be little reason to do so in view of the outcomes of past meetings. A dean of an arts and science college described his largely unsuccessful efforts to change the faculty attitude that students should "fish or cut bait." In rare contrast, a dean in a comprehensive university serving a predominantly minority student population reported offering an increased number of remedial sections and a reduction in class sizes.

The Problem of Underpreparation. In general, university faculty were less likely to be optimistic about their ability to work effectively with underprepared students than were their community college counterparts. One administrator, recently employed at a comprehensive university after serving in a community college for several years, attributed this difference to the fact that many community college faculty had taught in high school and had experience in working with a wider range of student abilities. From conversations with administrators, it was clear that faculty attitudes, particularly with respect to retention, represented a key barrier to the success of minority students.

Administrators in research universities did not talk about the need to alter faculty behaviors except in relation to their tightening standards for scholarships as this influenced tenure and promotion decisions. In contrast, administrators in comprehensive universities, much like their counterparts in community colleges, were optimistic about their ability to encourage faculty to become more sensitive to the needs of students in general and to those of minority students in particular. One comprehensive university in a relatively brief time span had changed from serving a predominantly white population to serving a predominantly minority population. The racial composition of its administrators, as might be expected, had changed much more rapidly than the racial composition of its faculty. White administrators expressed pessimism about the probability of changing the behavior of a predominantly white faculty, but minority administrators were convinced that the necessary changes would occur.

The single most effective strategy for producing changes in faculty attitudes toward minority students may well be the recruitment of minority faculty members. In a meeting between faculty members and one of the authors, the tone of a discussion was altered by the arrival of a black faculty member. Not only did she offer important insights into the needs of minority students, but her very presence elicited sensitivity to the issues of working with minority students from her nonminority colleagues.

Teaching of Writing Skills. Three levels of entry into the writing sequence were found in most of the universities studied. The first level involved the more or less standard two-course sequence that is traditionally part of the general education requirement. Below this standard sequence, a writing proficiency course was offered without degree credit; students exited from this course only after passing a competency examination. A third level involved a two-course sequence designed to prepare students for the entrance exam to the standard composition sequence.

The use of competency exams to assess students exiting from remedial courses or the standard composition sequence was a common practice. Two universities, one by state mandate and the other by action of its faculty senate, had recently initiated a standard examination to be taken by native students as well as community college transfers before they could receive junior status. The motivation for adopting the requirement was at least twofold. University faculty, as previously noted, were suspicious of the standards enforced in community colleges, but they were also concerned about the absence of writing requirements in their own upper-division courses amidst reports that their graduates lacked writing skills.

One research university had received a grant from the National Endowment for the Humanities to design a three-course writing sequence by bringing together teachers from high schools and adjacent community colleges with university faculty. The dean responsible for the program believed that this was the way to overcome suspicion about differences in standards and misunderstandings about the kinds of problems faced at the different levels of education. He observed, "Talking is not enough to alter the tendency faculty have for putting the blame for poor performance one level back." Interestingly, full-time faculty members in the English department of this university exhibited little enthusiasm for the project, perhaps because none were involved in teaching courses other than literature.

In the research universities, few, if any, writing courses were taught by full-time faculty. Instead, they were taught by graduate students and part-time faculty, sometimes recruited from adjacent community colleges. Several universities maintained a permanent cadre of lecturers, ineligible for tenure, to teach writing. Several offered graduate programs in teaching composition and rhetoric, and the graduate students from these programs served as the reservoir of needed talent for writing courses.

Perhaps the most interesting arrangement for handling remedial classes in writing involved a university that contracted with an adjacent community college to offer the classes, which would be taught by community college faculty, in university facilities. The community college claimed the student credit hours generated for state reimbursement while the university was also able to count the students as part of its enrollment since they were concurrently enrolled in other university courses. Most ingenious was the formal creation of a consortium between the university and the community college that permitted students with concurrent registration in both institutions to retain eligibility for financial aid.

In comprehensive universities where full-time faculty typically teach writing courses, teaching loads are lighter than in community colleges. Where faculty members taught composition exclusively, as occurred in predominantly minority institutions where the remedial load was unusually heavy, the maximum number of credit hours taught was nine, in contrast with the fifteen found in many community colleges. While community college faculty not infrequently teach composition classes in universities, the reverse is much less likely to occur, partly because research universities usually have restrictions against moonlighting by their faculty.

There was a sense among research university English faculty that minority students were not well served in their institutions, but there seemed to be little understanding of why this was the case. Nor did there seem to be much interest in exploring how the situation might be improved. Few minority students majored in English, and most English departments had few minority faculty members.

Mathematics. Many of the students who enter urban universities are poorly prepared in mathematics. The least selective comprehensive universities offered as many as five or six courses at precalculus levels. Some were as basic as "fundamental operations on whole numbers, decimals, and fractions." Others permitted "students in undergraduate programs which do not require a specific sequence in mathematics" to meet general education requirements with limited proficiency, although such students were still required to pass a mathematics examination. At the minimum, this examination could be passed by students having the equivalent of one year of high school algebra.

Less selective research universities typically offered two to four precalculus courses, which generally paralleled high school algebra, geometry, and trigonometry. More selective research universities offered one or two courses designed to cover the same high school content areas but in less time than their less selective counterparts. In research universities, precalculus courses were not accepted as a part of the degree programs of the high-demand majors, including business, engineering, and architecture.

Beyond the sequence designed to prepare students for calculus, math departments provided special courses for students in social sciences and other fields where advanced mathematical competencies were not required. But increasingly, the high-demand fields emphasized mathematics as an admission requirement. This emphasis, which sometimes exceeded the apparent need for mathematics in courses required by the major, seemed to reflect the confidence of university faculty in mathematics as an unchanging standard in an environment where there was constant pressure to adapt to students as they were rather than to require them to become what faculty believed they ought to be.

Mathematics clearly served a gatekeeper function for business, a major where student interest encouraged faculty to become as selective as their universities would tolerate. The explanation provided by faculty was that studies in business administration were becoming increasingly quantitative. While this assertion was undoubtedly accurate, it was given in the same institution where the business degree could also be earned by substituting a foreign language for the required math sequence.

It is difficult to criticize faculty for using mathematics as a screening tool, especially since quantitative concepts are involved in many advanced courses in high-demand areas and the preparation of those admitted was often meager. In one comprehensive university serving a predominantly minority population, only one-half of the entering students were able to pass the competency examination that measured the equivalent of eighth-grade arithmetic. Only 20 percent of those entering had the equivalent of one year of high school algebra or more. Even in the research universities, the number of students requiring some form of remediation in mathematics at entrance sometimes exceeded 50 percent.

The prognosis for those who enter remedial courses in mathematics generally was not good. The further behind they entered in the sequence, the more problematic it became. Attrition figures for entry-level mathematics courses ranged from 35 to 60 percent. The attrition figures for minorities in the one university that could provide these figures ranged from 15 to 25 percent higher than the class average. These figures did not apply to Asian students, who regularly outperform everyone, including nonminorities, in mathematics and the sciences. As one faculty member said, "Every mathematics professor dreams of a classroom full of Chinese."

Even those who do well in remedial courses are not guaranteed success in advanced courses. Faculty members from mathematics departments explained the poor performance in advanced courses of students coming out of their remedial sequence with the observation: "Student success in mathematics requires repeated exposures over time. You can't cram the amount of information required for these courses into one semester and expect students to retain enough to do them any good."

Like their colleagues in English departments, full-time faculty members in math distance themselves from remedial work. This generalization does not apply to comprehensive universities, where, as previously noted, as many as 80 percent of the entering students require some form of remedial assistance. In research universities, however, remedial courses were taught by part-time faculty, graduate students, or lecturers with nontenure track appointments. While the mathematics departments retained an oversight function, their involvement was as limited as possible.

Given the diversity among entering students and the varying competencies they present, these universities would seem to be an ideal setting for self-paced learning. Indeed, many did use self-pacing for entry-level courses, but this seemed more a way of managing large numbers of students than a strategy for promoting student success. In one comprehensive university where tutors had been withdrawn from self-paced classrooms as an economy measure, faculty members responded by placing more emphasis on lectures, discussions, and individual assistance from faculty members. The increased structure and restrictions on the number of times students could repeat examinations increased their success ratios. This experience was reported in other settings as well, suggesting that self-paced learning has limited value for underprepared students in mathematics for the same reason that learning strategies based on technology fail in community colleges. Seriously underprepared students from educationally disadvantaged backgrounds require structure and human support. Providing these does not guarantee success, but it does improve the odds.

University math faculty members displayed a curious ambivalence in their attitudes toward working with underprepared students. On the one hand, they stated that such students should go to community colleges; on the other hand, they suggested that students coming directly to the university received a better preparation than those beginning in community colleges. Their ambivalence was also reflected in policies for working with transfer students. Despite articulation agreements and the absence of any statistical evidence favoring the performance of native students over community college transfers, courses below the level of calculus were not recognized in university placement procedures. All students entering as transfers who had not completed calculus were required to take a placement examination and were placed according to the examination rather than on the basis of courses completed at the community college.

It was difficult to escape the conclusion that blacks and Hispanics were being systematically channeled into "soft" majors because of their mathematics backgrounds. Mathematics faculty members reported that these minorities did not do well in math courses either as transfers or as freshmen. Faculty also reported fewer minority students in remedial courses, partly reflecting new admissions standards that have reduced the number of minorities being admitted.

Improving math skills among minority students emerged as one of the most important strategies for increasing the number of baccalaureate graduates. But it was difficult to see how this could be accomplished without reforming the elementary and secondary school programs through which students entered. None of the universities were very optimistic about the effectiveness of remedial education in compensating for poor preparation in the public schools.

Choice of Majors by Community College Transfers. Most transfers enter urban universities from community colleges in fields such as human services, social services, speech, and the administration of justice. The percentage of minorities is highest in colleges of arts and sciences. Of course, many are there because they have been denied admission to the program of their choice. A major challenge for arts and science colleges is how to advise students who want to be in another college. One strategy that has been tried without much success is to encourage all students to meet degree requirements for the college of arts and sciences. Clearly, arts and science colleges serve a community college function within the university, as evidenced by a report from one dean. When funding cutbacks forced tightening of what had been fairly modest admission requirements, one student who was turned away commented, "You mean we can't even get into liberal arts?"

The practices in oversubscribed colleges such as business and engineering contrast sharply with those in colleges of arts and sciences. In one university, all transfer students were expected to complete a prebusiness sequence before being considered for admission to the college of business. The sequence required that they pass four courses in the major with a minimum grade point average of 2.25. Despite more restrictive admission policies than arts and science colleges, however, business colleges reported a relatively high ratio of minorities to nonminorities and numbered among their majors more transfer than native students. Business college administrators with the best access to performance data reported that the problems of success for transfer minority students were no different from those for native minority students. One associate dean noted that it did not make much difference where students did their lower-division work, except in the area of accounting. He added, "Our faculty have set high standards and require a lot from students."

Engineering schools had more facts and figures about their students than did most other colleges. They were also more likely to have independent programs aimed at recruiting minorities. Such programs operated both at national and regional levels. The leadership shown in this area by colleges of engineering seemed related in part to the extremely small number of minorities enrolled in their programs. In several universities where the overall enrollment of blacks and Hispanics ranged from 10 percent to 15 percent, only 2 to 6 percent of them were enrolled in engineering.

An exception to this general underrepresentation was reported in a companion study (Bender and Chalfont-Thomas, 1986), where the proportion of minority students enrolled in a school of engineering exceeded by three times their proportion in the university as a whole, despite the use of more selective admissions criteria for engineering. The success of this school in attracting minority students was attributed by the dean to an array of initiatives with high schools and community colleges. Identified as key factors in these initiatives were the recruitment of minority faculty members and the use of peer students as role models.

In most universities, however, both minority and transfer students were underrepresented. In one university where transfer students accounted for more than 60 percent of the university enrollment, they represented only 23 percent of the enrollment in the engineering school. One reason most engineering schools do not recruit transfer students is the view that the preparation battle for engineering is won or lost in junior high school.

Despite the relative absence of recruiting programs aimed at community colleges, even the more selective engineering schools enrolled transfers from a wide range of community colleges, including inner-city institutions that served predominantly minority student populations and did not offer engineering transfer programs. Summer programs emphasizing skill development and motivation were a common approach to the recruitment of minority high school students. Yet urban universities were not necessarily the beneficiaries of these recruiting efforts. One dean who had considerable experience with summer programs commented, "Any student who qualifies for our college as a result of a summer program also qualifies for other programs that offer more status and where there are residence halls."

One imaginative effort to improve recruiting from inner-city community colleges involved a cooperative program through which minority students expressing an interest in engineering were given special opportunities for enrichment and assistance and guaranteed three opportunities to be considered for admission, each time in a preferred status if program requirements were met. In general, where universities have developed programs with community colleges, the results have been satisfactory. One dean noted that all the minorities who persisted in his program after a year were either transfers or had taken part in the university's own special program.

Cooperative programs between community colleges and universities seemed to be the exception rather than the rule. Where they did exist, it was unusual to find them focused on inner-city clientele. California, with its state-funded transfer centers, appears to be doing more in this area than most other states. A university with an inner-city location in a different state taught special advanced level engineering courses for community college students in the neighboring suburbs. When asked why such courses were not taught in the city, an administrator responded, "The numbers aren't there."

Student Services

Research universities typically did not offer the extensive support services found in community colleges and to a lesser extent in comprehensive universities, especially those serving a predominantly minority student body. Within research universities there was much less evidence of concern about minority or underprepared students. Most were committed to accepting losses in enrollment as the preferred alternative to retaining students who did not meet their admissions criteria. Within research universities academic support services such as tutoring, remedial courses, and skills laboratories were usually linked to student affairs rather than to the educational program. Regardless of where the services reported, however, there appeared to be little concern about integrating activities; as one result, efforts to serve minority students seemed excessively fragmented.

Comprehensive universities located in urban centers followed practices that resembled those in community colleges rather than those in research universities. They differed primarily in placing greater emphasis on exit competencies and in being less flexible in adapting practices to the behavior patterns of their students. Neither comprehensive universities nor research universities produced well-articulated philosophies about the needs of urban minorities or how these could best be met. The one exception was the minority president of a comprehensive university who defined a philosophical position that he carefully linked to a comprehensive program of services provided by the university.

Admission Requirements. These have been stiffened in most universities during the past four or five years. The rationale for increasing such requirements, as stated by one university vice-president, underscores a value separating community colleges and universities:

> We were in a dangerous situation in terms of the students we admitted; ACT scores were below national averages. We were spending money on support systems without evident returns, and student quality had begun to affect what was happening in the classrooms.

Institutions were well aware of the effect of higher admission standards on minority enrollments. When one group of faculty was asked how they would preserve access while improving quality, the response of the department chair was, "That's like cutting the deficit without raising taxes."

Most universities did not expect their enrollments to decline overall as a result of higher admission standards. At the same time, there was little tendency to back away from increased requirements even where actual declines had taken place. Faculty members and administrators stressed their readiness to accept declining enrollments if necessary to avoid reducing the quality of instruction. The preferred strategy, however, was to offset declines in undergraduate enrollments by increasing the number of graduate students.

In addition to the strategy of increasing graduate enrollments, administrators in a number of urban universities compensated for the decline in students who entered directly from high school by admitting more transfer students. Some universities accepted transfers from community colleges who would not have been admissible on the basis of high school performance or test scores. Such students typically needed only nine to eighteen hours of credit and a grade point average of 2.0. Because there were no distribution requirements, nonadmissible high school graduates were able to enroll in the least demanding courses at the community college but still meet the requirements for university admission.

Just as the use of selective admission standards for high-demand, high-cost programs in an institution committed to open access constitutes one of the great paradoxes of the urban community college, so does the practice of near-open admissions at the junior level, combined with more selective admissions for freshmen, constitute a paradox for many urban universities. And there is growing evidence that the impact on the quality of upper-division offerings in the "open-door" university majors may be very similar to the impact of underprepared matriculants on the transfer curriculum in community colleges. An editorial in the student newspaper of one university written by a business major identified conditions in upper-division courses almost identical to those found in a study of a community college (Richardson, Fisk, and Okun, 1983).

Even with high school graduates, most urban universities

set only modest admission standards. One required students to rank in the upper two-thirds of their high school graduating classes and to present acceptable test scores. Another university by law was required to admit all graduates of state high schools who had completed a college preparatory curriculum. Both of these universities had extensive remedial programs and perceived themselves as competing with community colleges for the same students, a perception shared by the community college administrators in their respective cities.

Universities followed a two-step process in notifying transfer students of the number of community college credits for which they would receive credit. The admissions letter reported the number of hours earned in courses recognized by the university but also stated that acceptance to the program of choice and the evaluation of transfer credits applicable to a degree program would be determined by the school or college responsible for the program. Thus students received two separate and sometimes conflicting communications about their status and the applicability of work completed before transferring.

At the college or department level, admission practices varied in relation to student enrollment pressures. In high-demand areas, the admissions process took longer and frequently resulted in fewer credits being accepted as meeting the requirements for a degree. Students routinely found themselves with more elective credits than required and fewer credits in the major than anticipated. In several universities, those knowledgeable about the transcript evaluation process reported that, regardless of the number of hours earned before transferring, the typical matriculant who had completed two years in a community college would require an additional three years to earn the baccalaureate degree.

Recruiting. The emphasis in university recruiting remains on the recent high school graduate, but the reality of matriculation demographics causes many less selective universities to concentrate on the transfer student and the part-time adult student. Most universities with predominantly nonminority student populations reported concentrating most of their efforts on high schools and community colleges in the surrounding suburbs. Inner-city public schools received very little attention from university recruiters except for contacts from those representing special programs for minorities. One university that had previously held special registrations on an inner-city community college campus discontinued the practice. The reason given was that the effort had led to the admission of only a few students. Typically, each university admissions office had one minority staff member who maintained linkages with schools that were viewed as potential sources of minority students.

University officials were quite candid about their reasons for not placing more emphasis on the recruitment of minority students. First, the urban universities already enrolled the highest proportions of minority students of all institutions in their respective systems; thus, there was little external pressure for increasing the number of such students. Second, most policy-level administrators in the less prestigious universities were pessimistic about their ability to recruit well-qualified minority students. One admissions officer summed it up this way: "We don't stand a chance of getting really able black students; those who are able are recruited heavily by schools with more money and more status." Finally, many in the universities questioned the wisdom of expending scarce resources on support programs that did not improve success for any significant percentage of the students enrolled. In addition, there was concern that emphasis on these programs might contribute to status and image problems within their respective systems.

Contributing to the reluctance to emphasize minorities in recruitment efforts was the perception that the products of city public schools were poorly prepared for college. One administrator noted that the superintendent of schools had written off the current crop of students as unsalvageable. Another university administrator observed that the public schools were so politicized and understaffed as to be little more than custodial agencies. Perceptions of the products of inner-city community colleges were little better. The prevailing judgment seemed to be that research universities could not achieve their objectives by recruiting minority students from city public school systems or urban community college districts. One administrator noted,

"The numbers of quality minority students just aren't there." In fairness to those who held these perceptions, an examination of data on multicultural and predominantly minority high schools in one city revealed a very small number of students who met the admissions criteria of the highly selective urban university in that city.

Orientation. Practices here ran the gamut from a one-hour standard slide presentation of university services to an elaborate two-day program, complete with social activities and small-group sessions focused on strategies for adjusting to university life and succeeding in studies. The more elaborate programs were offered by universities that appeared to be the most committed to minority student achievement. Provisions were made in all universities for student advising, but the quality of advising was far from uniform.

In one university, an administrator noted that its advising system received poor grades because many of its students came from community colleges with a student development emphasis while the university's own faculty members were not student centered. Later in the same conversation, she expanded on her point: "The faculty here believe there are too many students, and they don't have the time to advise them. For some faculty, advising means putting out a supply of stamped forms in front of their office door."

In a different situation, a minority staff member responsible for a student advising program described a recurring scene at the faculty senate meeting:

> Whenever someone points out that advising isn't very good at this university, some faculty member always observes that advising isn't very good because faculty aren't paid to do it. At this point, the president becomes angry and lectures those present that faculty are expected to teach and advise; but the faculty are never persuaded.

Several universities held special orientation programs for minority students that were planned and supervised by minority staff members responsible for special support programs. Students attending had to meet special eligibility requirements because of the use of categorical funds. A number of universities offered orientation sessions covering such standard topics as student services, campus life, and university requirements for transfer students. Getting minority and transfer students to attend special sessions was a challenge. One university that combined orientation for transfer students with early registration for courses reported that only 15 percent of those eligible participated. The comprehensive university that seemed to work the hardest at encouraging minority students to attend attracted only about a third of the eligible pool. The tendency for transfers and minorities to make late decisions about attending contributed heavily to the problem of getting them to participate in orientation sessions and to register early enough to be assured some reasonable selection of classes.

As was true of admissions, freshman students received the most attention, transfers into the day program came next, and evening students received the least. In talking about advising, one faculty member noted, "There is an office which advises evening students and other unusual students." Later, it became clear that the category of unusual students included transfers. Another faculty member in the group noted that advising for freshmen was more systematic and better organized than for transfers: "Transfer students drift in and are welcomed with open arms, but not helped at all." Another faculty member added, "Most of our majors are transfers, but they are not minorities or community college transfers."

The basic assumption undergirding orientation activities was that students had defined educational objectives and only needed assistance in selecting courses to achieve those objectives. While the quality of advising as assessed by the institutions themselves ranged from poor to no better than adequate, it was apparent that a student who sought out advising services would find them. It was not as apparent that efforts were made to ensure that transfer students learned about the importance of advising or were encouraged to take advantage of this service.

Assessment and Placement. Urban universities experienced many of the same problems in these areas as did community colleges. Students arrived late and had to be placed in classes before they had completed prescribed assessment procedures. The influx of underprepared students in the least selective institutions placed pressure on faculty to adapt course requirements to avoid excessive attrition. As in community colleges, students were not allowed to enroll in math, English, chemistry, and computer science unless they had completed the assessment process. In some universities, however, they were permitted to enroll in other courses for which they lacked prerequisite skills. The practice of permitting underprepared students to enroll in regular university courses without providing them with the supportive services found in community colleges did much to explain the high attrition figures for minority students who entered as native freshmen.

Placement examinations were routinely administered in reading, writing, and mathematics to all freshmen. In some institutions, study skills and career interests were also assessed. Transfer students were tested in reading and writing if they had not completed the English composition sequence. Several universities had either placed one course in the composition sequence at the junior level or were planning to do so as a strategy for ensuring that no community college transfer would complete requirements for a university degree without undergoing an assessment of writing skills by university personnel. In addition, transfer students were tested in mathematics if they had not completed a course in calculus and were then placed without regard to math courses taken at the community college. One faculty member explained the practice this way: "Transfer course descriptions sound fine in the catalogue, but when we get people here, they just don't know the materials." From the perspective of university faculty members, transfer students presented at least as much of an assessment problem as did entering freshmen.

Faculty members in such popular majors as engineering, business, and health-related professions had developed additional safeguards against admitting underprepared transfer students. Departments within these fields administered validation examinations or withheld credit until the subsequent course in a sequence was completed. In several universities, transfer students were admitted as arts and science majors and required to complete a minimum of twelve credits in specified courses before learning whether they would be accepted in the program of their choice. While this approach was not significantly different from the one followed by community colleges in admitting students to their own health-related career programs, the impact was to encourage early transfer, a practice that has been found in many settings to be detrimental to student persistence.

Like research institutions, comprehensive universities wanted to raise their standards and achieve the marks of respectability conferred by specialized accreditation in areas such as business and nursing. At the same time, they were more committed to their students and to maintaining what one dean described as "a concerned and loving environment." Their emphasis on the use of examinations to validate competencies reflected the philosophy expressed by one administrator: "I'm not interested in who comes in; I'm interested in the competencies of those that exit." Motivation as a variable contributing to student success received the same attention in universities with minority leadership as it did in community colleges serving minority populations.

Financial Assistance. Most public universities administered very little of their own financial assistance. The exceptions were universities concerned about increasing the number of qualified minority students either because of strong commitment from their leaders or because of the requirements of a state desegregation plan. The percentage of students receiving financial aid ranged from 22 percent in a predominantly white university located in an area away from the inner city not well served by public transportation to more than 85 percent in a predominantly black university serving an inner-city population. As with community colleges, the percentage of students receiving financial aid was highly correlated with the percentage of minority students in attendance.

Work study was an important component of most financial aid programs. A research university with an advantageous location in a suburban area between two major cities reported placing 9,000 students or almost half of its total enrollment each year; many of the jobs were provided by employers other than the university itself. This university expected students on financial aid to earn a minimum of 50 percent of their entitlement.

In another instance, an inner-city university located in the heart of a black residential area was heavily dependent on student work-study funds. Of the 1,000 students eligible for the program and willing to participate, only 400 could be funded. Given limitations on the availability of grants and work study, there was growing concern about the extent to which students had to rely on loans. One financial aid officer noted, "Every time we increase tuition and fees, students must borrow more money." With the publication of a recent congressional report, it has become clear that the concerns of this officer were well justified (Evangelauf, 1987).

Urban universities experienced the same problem as community colleges in keeping students eligible for financial assistance. But their responses were generally less flexible, partly because of concern about their ability to provide adequate services and appropriate courses for late arrivals. In one comprehensive university, students were able to count three noncredit remedial courses in maintaining eligibility for state financial aid. If a student did not pass a required competency exam after the first try, the course had to be repeated as an overload. This policy demonstrated one advantage for underprepared students attending community colleges; namely, a transfer student who uses remedial courses to maintain eligibility at a community college can retake the remedial sequence in the university without losing eligibility for financial assistance.

Community college transfers were notorious for making late decisions. Just as it handicapped them in course selection and advising, it also resulted in their receiving less financial aid than they might have been eligible for. University requirements that bills be paid following preregistration to avoid cancellation of course reservations compounded the problem. For most universities, bills had to be paid several months in advance of the beginning of a semester to ensure an appropriate selection of courses. Apart from the financial strains caused by this practice, there seemed to be no systematic way of communicating this information to new transfer students.

To cope with this problem, most universities allowed students who could present a student aid report establishing their eligibility for a Pell grant to complete registration without payment of fees. Less frequently, special arrangements were available to extend credit for the purchase of books and necessary supplies. One university reported changing a policy that had permitted use of institutional funds to help students who had difficulty qualifying for financial assistance after experience showed that those who arrived late typically left early, with the university left holding a worthless note.

Strategies for Improving Student Achievement

Universities, like community colleges, have developed various strategies to improve student opportunities for success. The strategies reported here include interventions that universities would implement if they had additional resources as well as those already in effect.

High Schools. There was practically universal recognition that early identification of potential college students was important and that preparation during high school years needed to be strengthened. One of the ways universities attempted to strengthen communication links with high schools that served predominantly minority student populations was by assigning minority staff members as liaison persons. There was also agreement that university faculty needed to become more aware of conditions in the public schools from which minority students graduated. The prescription was a simple one: Get faculty more involved in the schools and in the communities they serve. But as in the case of the mice who decided to "bell the cat," there was considerable question about how this desirable objective should be achieved. One university provided a good example of how not to do it. It scheduled an all-day seminar on the retention of black students but failed to invite any of its own black students to the meeting.

A flagship university located in a relatively urban state

capital reported a faculty-initiated program of considerable promise. Concerned about a deteriorating situation in the public schools attended by their children, faculty members volunteered their time as consultants on the curriculum and as unpaid instructors of enrichment classes for teachers and students. The result was described as a "renaissance" of the public schools. Unfortunately, many faculty members who teach in urban universities do not reside in the school districts from which their more disadvantaged students matriculate.

In working with high school students, universities placed considerable emphasis on increasing motivation and getting students socially involved. Summer challenge programs provided high school students with an intensive experience in academics and group life at many universities. Invitations to cultural and athletic events helped ease the social transition. The director of a special program for minorities in one university conducted seminars for high school students to assist them in improving their scores on the American College Test (ACT). She also offered seminars to help students present themselves in the best possible light to universities that they were interested in attending. She advised universities to "be aggressive, they cannot wait for minority students to come to them."

University staff suggested that minority high school students should be urged to apply early and to register early and that they should be encouraged to go into fields other than the social sciences. Special programs should be developed to help them use libraries effectively. Finally, staff in one university suggested that the state coordinating board should take the leadership in encouraging the establishment of programs in high schools to give minorities better guidance, particularly in the year before they go to college.

Community Colleges. Perhaps the most noteworthy aspect of university strategies for working with urban community colleges was their relative scarcity. The small number of such strategies reported was particularly puzzling given the fact that more than half the students on urban university campuses get there by way of transfer. The only strategy mentioned by more than one university involved articulation meetings that brought faculty from community colleges face-to-face with their university colleagues. Such meetings occurred in half the cities involved in the study and took three basic forms. In the first, a single meeting for the university system was hosted each year by a different university campus. These meetings involved exchange of information on student performance and discussion of system-level articulation issues, but they were not designed to encourage contact between faculty members at the college or department level.

A second variation involved a meeting hosted by a single university for its major feeder community colleges. In the best example of this type of meeting, the morning was devoted to a discussion of institutionwide concerns. In the afternoon, faculty members and counselors were hosted by the colleges to which their specializations most closely related, and the meetings became working sessions on articulation issues at the department levels.

The third, and in many respects most promising, form, involved establishment of an articulation committee under the joint auspices of a university governing board and a community college governing board. The articulation committee was given authority to appoint working committees of faculty members from universities and community colleges in any discipline where articulation problems were seen to exist. These committees in turn were charged with defining the nature of the problem more precisely and proposing a solution to their respective statewide boards for implementation.

A different strategy used with mixed results in one state involved the definition of core curricula in majors under the leadership of the state coordinating board. Those who supported this approach indicated that students who adhered closely to the core curriculum experienced few problems in transferring. Critics, however, felt that the approach was time consuming, that the results went out-of-date quickly or were ignored by many of the four-year institutions, and that the alternative of defining a single general education transfer program would have been preferable.

Categorically Funded Programs. The federal government and a number of states have special programs focused on educationally disadvantaged students who meet any two of three criteria: they are first-generation college students, they come from low-income families, or they are handicapped. Most urban universities receive funding for such programs, which are often organized as a microcosm of the university. Typically, they provide such services as recruiting, counseling, tutoring, and basic skills courses in math and English. The courses carry administrative credit to keep students eligible for financial aid but may not be counted toward graduation. One minority administrator responsible for directing such a special program summarized it as "the way the university discharges its responsibilities to minority students."

Those responsible for special programs reported enrollments of minority students from two to four times the representation of minority students in the rest of the university. In part, this occurred because special-program staff often had responsibility for advising on admissions in the "differentially qualified" entering student category. Program directors provided studies demonstrating that underprepared students enrolled in their programs achieved success at rates significantly higher than similarly qualified students who entered the university without enrolling in their programs. Special programs appeared to be generally well accepted by other members of the university community. But the reported effectiveness of these programs and their acceptance did not seem to motivate most universities to invest their own resources in making them available to a greater number of students.

Not the least important of the contributions of the special programs is the minority staff they bring to the university. Beyond conducting special programs, this staff provides an important channel of communication between the university and counselors and students in predominantly minority high schools and community colleges.

Support Services. While many support services for minority students were provided through the special programs described above, not all minority students entered through the special-program route. And the problems of retention were by no means limited to minority students. One urban university reported that after the fall semester, 40 percent of all entering students would be gone from the university. Universities tolerated the revolving door phenomenon as long as each new year produced replacements for the students who did not return. But that is no longer the case, and universities are giving increased attention to activities designed to improve retention for all students.

In one university, a counseling center responding to a special committee on recruitment and retention designed a comprehensive student assessment program to help students identify strengths and weaknesses in skills necessary to academic success. In addition to providing an extensive program of career planning, the counseling center focused on helping students plan strategies for coping successfully with the university environment. The center offered a wide range of self-help, noncredit courses and focused on native freshmen. Transfer students were not excluded from participation, but neither was there any systematic effort to involve them.

There was nearly universal agreement among representatives of participating universities on the importance of residence halls for improving opportunities for minority students. Those universities that had residence halls reported disproportionate numbers of minority students living there. Those universities lacking residence halls commonly had plans to request such facilities under the rationale that urban students in general and minority students in particular needed alternatives to living at home in order to improve their chances of succeeding.

Academic Programs. Faculty members were not unaware of the problems experienced by minority students, and many were sympathetic to improving opportunities for them. But the small number of minority faculty and the lack of experience of nonminority faculty in dealing with minority students limited the strategies devised and led to disagreements about which, if any, were most likely to succeed. One college of arts and science made the decision to implement two recommendations of an internal task force because, as the dean candidly admitted, "There was some reason to believe they might be effective, and they were cheap." This college, one of the few willing to spend its own money on the problem, provided evidence of the peril of combining limited expertise and bargain-basement approaches. One program involved paying a good student to take notes in a class and to conduct a seminar to which other students could come for review and to check the accuracy of their own notes. As of the eighth week of the semester, no minorities had participated in these seminars, but then neither had very many nonminorities.

An academic strategy mentioned twice by chief executive officers, neither of whom had had much success in selling the concept to their faculties, involved the establishment of a general or basic college into which all entering students would go until they had demonstrated a level of proficiency necessary for admission to the college of their choice. Both of the institutions where the strategy was mentioned admitted large numbers of unprepared students and attempted to serve them with very limited resources. Both had vestibule programs to which students not meeting criteria for admission to a college were assigned. Neither of these vestibule programs was perceived by anyone, including the presidents, as particularly effective. In one of the two, the assignment to the vestibule program was seen as a punishment, a perception well supported by the program description, which was under revision at the time of the site visit. The estimate was that no more than 10 percent of those entering this program ever graduated from the university.

The more selective research universities typically did not offer vestibule programs except for courses and services provided under categorically funded special programs. As an alternative, they emphasized faculty advising and mentoring as key strategies. In particular, emphasis was placed on bringing minority students into contact with role models through an advising or mentoring process. Students were also monitored closely; warning letters were sent to those who dropped below a 2.5 grade point average or who earned less than a *C* in any course. The letters urged students to meet with a university adviser or to take advantage of other available assistance.

Conclusion

For all research universities, hiring more minority faculty members and administrators was seen as the most crucial step in making them more hospitable to black and Hispanic students. A minority staff member in one predominantly white university summed it up by saying, "A major way to retain students is to let them know that the university cares about them through recruiting faculty members and training peer advisers to be certain that every minority student has at least one other minority person at the campus with whom to interact." Another staff member from the same institution added, "We need to show minority students that it is possible for a minority person to achieve in this environment. Currently, no one speaks for minority concerns in senior councils; as a result, they are seen as just one more special-interest group and treated accordingly." This large university, serving an urban area heavily populated by minorities, employed only three minority persons in reasonably senior positions: an associate dean, an assistant dean, and one full professor.

While faculty members in all universities suggested strategies such as providing more remedial courses or additional tutorial services and permitting students to declare academic bankruptcy, the most coherent set of principles was articulated by a comprehensive university that served a predominantly minority student population. The advice it provided gives evidence of its experience in working with large numbers of underprepared students in an inner-city setting. The university's suggestions were to (1) provide a good orientation program with strong follow-up contact beyond the first session; (2) use proficiency exams to force students to confront deficiencies and deal with them early in their college careers; (3) monitor student progress closely and intervene as soon as problems appear; (4) make the entire staff as accessible as possible to students; (5) provide tutoring that is linked with classes; (6) enforce explicit standards of progress tied to appropriate regulations for dismissal; (7) make certain that registration procedures are designed to prevent students from enrolling in classes that they are not prepared to take; (8) encourage close working relationships between the counseling and special-program staffs so that students' needs can be assessed comprehensively and programs to assist them can be cooperatively defined; (9) encourage the development of strong student organizations to provide cohesive groups with whom students can identify.

Administrative commitment was evident among universities that reported progress in improving the success rates of minority students. Administrators in such institutions used resources to support specific interventions, in addition to expressing support for programs aimed at minority students in speeches and written documents. In one university, the president promised to increase the expense budget of any department that hired a black faculty member by 10 percent. Two departments hired black faculty members shortly after this offer was made.

Unfortunately, however, excessive fragmentation limits the effectiveness of many special programs for minority students. In one university, separate programs for Hispanics, American Indians, and blacks reported individually to the academic vice-president but were not coordinated with university counseling services, the office of admissions, or with one another. The programs helped minority students but did not achieve the results evident in the previously mentioned comprehensive university, where the president communicated an institutional commitment to an organized and systematic effort to help minority students succeed.

Urban universities provide important opportunities for educationally disadvantaged students, offer many special assistance programs of high quality, and number among their faculty and staffs many individuals strongly committed to improving access. But the conflicting priorities they experience in an environment of constrained resources is reflected in their ambivalence about what they can do for marginally prepared students and what they should do for them. The moral imperative to improve educational opportunities as a means of promoting social justice conflicts with the cultural ideal of the self-directed and independent learner functioning as a contributing member of a community of scholars. Since the direction chosen by urban universities in responding to these conflicting pressures is influenced by the context provided by their state systems of higher education, we turn our attention to this area in the following chapter.

5

The States' Role in Improving Minority Education

State legislatures have been hard pressed by the rapidity and nature of change in all aspects of society in recent years. Advocates for a wide range of social services initiated with federal support now seek state funding in response to current or anticipated shifts in federal priorities. Blue-ribbon citizen committees, legislative task forces, and studies mandated by state agencies have created a variety of reforms that ultimately will have an impact on all levels of education. In some states legislators have mandated assessment of elementary and secondary school performance. In others basic skills tests have been mandated for any student entering teacher-training programs.

The initial results of testing programs at all levels have been devastating for blacks, Hispanics, and Native Americans, who have placed significantly below their nonminority peers. Charges of racial discrimination, cultural bias, de facto segregation, and the reduction of the number of minority teachers in the classroom have been advanced by national and local minority advocacy organizations, including the NAACP. Court challenges have occurred in several states, but the U.S. Supreme

Court has ruled that such testing is an appropriate use of state authority. In several states, legislators have mandated course content in the public high schools, placing emphasis on English, mathematics, science, and computer literacy. In at least one state, high school academic programs must include courses comparable to those required under the old Carnegie unit plan for high schools, including at least four years of English, three years of math, two years of social science, two years of physical science, and two years of foreign language.

Legislative concern for higher education centers on issues involving quality. For many legislators quality means establishing more selective admission standards as reflected in higher ACT and SAT test scores and improved high school grade point averages. This same concern may also extend to course offerings. In one state, the legislature prohibits universities from offering remedial programs and calls for them to contract with public community colleges for the remediation requirements of the freshman class. Funds are made available to accomplish this design. Another approach has been to require academic skills tests to be administered as part of the admissions and placement process and again during the sophomore year before students move to the upper division. These tests typically are given for several years on a pilot basis as part of a transition strategy to permit students in the pipeline to have the benefit of a grace period to benefit from instructional reforms within colleges and universities.

Legislators are concerned with the impact of these reforms on minority students. Several states have provided for "exception rules" whereby institutions are permitted to waive cutoff scores and other adverse indicators for students otherwise judged qualified to benefit from the program of studies. Characteristically, the exception rule applies for up to 10 percent of any class enrolled. *Adams* v. *Richardson* states and those with similar court mandates have elaborate plans for improving racial balance among previously segregated institutions. Desegregation plans include extensive reporting procedures and make additional demands for funding on already constrained state budgets.

Prominent but of lesser priority among legislative concerns is the condition of private higher education. The general view is that the public sector is overbuilt and that the balance between private and public institutions is thus in jeopardy. Several actions of legislatures have been directed at this concern, including financial aid programs to provide tuition equalization and provisions for program contracting with individual private colleges and universities either on the basis of the number of state residents in attendance or on a program basis in such costly areas as medical education, high-tech engineering programs, and similar fields.

State Coordinating Board Priorities and Strategies

College and university responses to the concerns of governors, legislators, and other actors on the state scene are mediated by statewide coordinating and governing boards. While their authority varies according to state law and custom, such boards in general exercise responsibility for planning, budget review, and approval of new academic programs (Millett, 1984). They may also be assigned responsibility for collecting data and reporting, reviewing existing academic programs for quality or unnecessary duplication, monitoring compliance with affirmative action, and conducting legislatively authorized studies or programs. While the authority of statewide boards participating in this study ranged from advisory to governing, we have used the term *coordinating board* to refer to all in the interests of avoiding the identification of specific states.

The priorities for higher education that have emerged among state coordinating boards in response to legislative concerns are remarkably similar. One that appears high on most lists is improved articulation between universities and the public schools. This priority is a natural outgrowth of the emphasis that legislatures are placing on higher university admission standards.

A second common priority focuses on economic development. In the Frost Belt states, the emphasis is typically on retraining. In the Sun Belt states, the emphasis is on attracting new industry. In both cases, high tech seems to be the preferred industry. Research universities tend to communicate and interact with key members of the executive and legislative branches in this pursuit, but community colleges are more likely to look to the coordinating agency for appropriate inclusion in planning.

A third priority, described in one state as "selective excellence" and in another as "quality improvement," is designed to encourage each institution to build on existing strengths by replacing the traditional search for commonalities (which has driven much budget development activity in the past) with a search for unique strengths. As one state official observed, "If all of our public colleges and universities are emphasizing the same things, then we probably have too many of them."

Concerns About Minority Student Achievement. The safest generalization about minority student achievement is that if it is not already a priority in a given state, it is likely to soon become one. The states differ more in their ability to describe the extent of the problem than in their strategies for dealing with it. The most focused and comprehensive strategies were reported by states with good data on student achievement, disaggregated by race. Other states were cognizant of the need to collect such data but in its absence were less knowledgeable about the issue and more tentative about priorities and approaches.

In a state with a good data base, the issue was described as a "pipeline problem" in reference to the large number of minority students who drop out before graduating from high school. The coordinating agency had been working actively with the state's department of education to promote reforms within the public schools. Promotion campaigns aimed at minorities were designed to encourage completion of high school, enrollment in academic college preparatory programs, and emphasis on math and science. Promotional literature, media spots, and statewide conferences were among the activities sponsored.

In a state with a high concern about minority student achievement, a major independent report prepared for a legislative committee provoked a sharp controversy over the data used to describe the problems of minority achievement in the state's largest city. Within this state, there have also been two major reports on the issue presented to the coordinating board by its own staff.

A third state offered three different legislative programs that directly or indirectly were designed to enhance achievement for minority students. One focused on the assessment of basic skills and concomitant funding for instructional programs in basic skills, a second established a fund for institutional initiatives aimed at equalizing opportunity, and a third provided grants to increase minority enrollment and degree completion. Significantly, much of the credit for these programs was given to the state chancellor, who used a combination of diligent effort and personal diplomacy to secure the programs from the legislature while encouraging institutions to respond to them as a priority.

A fourth state provides grants to public institutions to equalize educational opportunity through programs that improve minority student achievement. In 1983, the coordinating board for this state authorized community colleges to earmark up to 10 percent of staff and program development funds for minority initiatives. Community colleges are required to demonstrate that the initiatives for which such funds are used do in fact benefit minority students.

In a fifth state, where concerns about minority participation and achievement are spelled out in a desegregation plan, a state official used national statistics whenever he discussed minority groups; this reflected the very limited data that the agency had collected from its own institutions. Without being asked, the same official denied that the board had relegated minority students to community colleges: "We are falsely accused of relegating minorities to the community colleges. We are not relegating minorities! Minority students choose the community college themselves because they are job oriented; the community college is the right place for them, and it is performing an important service."

Beyond providing incentive grants and conducting special studies, some states sponsored staff development programs. In one state, workshops were conducted on the retention of minority students. These workshops have been less effective than anticipated because of the low level of participation by senior colleges and universities and the representatives selected for involvement. The agency official responsible for conducting the workshops commented, "Originally, we had hoped to have more senior administrators and faculty and, of course, both universities and community colleges [represented]. Not only are community colleges more likely to be represented, but student personnel officers are the most frequent attendees." The practice of delegating responsibilities for improving opportunities for minorities to student affairs administrators seemed to be pervasive at both state and institutional levels.

Minority members of coordinating board staffs frequently shared the views of their institutional colleagues on appropriate strategies for improving minority student achievement. In contrast to the position of most coordinating boards on residence halls for urban universities, a minority staff member argued, "Dorms are really important because they produce stability and a support structure where common values related to achievement can be experienced." A black vice-chancellor in another state described his solution to the plight of urban blacks:

> What is needed is the creation of residential schools for urban minorities. They need to escape from the present environment, which is debilitating, even if they must be taken from the family. Even our best urban schools can't compensate for the neighborhood environment and the street culture in which these kids live.

Among other strategies proposed by minority staff members were special preservice and inservice faculty training to make them aware of the minority student as a nontraditional learner, collegiate institutions adopting an urban school where faculty would work in the reality of the public school setting, and initiatives among the urban minority communities to raise the overall educational values and traditions of their people.

Articulation as a State Priority. With some prominent exceptions, articulation between community colleges and universities has not been accorded the same priority as articulation with high schools, economic development, or "selective excellence" (discussed above). As one individual put it, "Articulation is not the wheel that squeaks the loudest." The basic coordinating board position on articulation was stated by another official: "Our board believes that any student with an associate degree should be able to transfer to any four-year institution in this state." Then he added, "This is a position that is easy to state but hard to implement; it is beginning to create conflict with some other board objectives."

Even though the articulation wheel does not squeak the loudest, most state coordinating agencies give at least some attention to the issue. Most will intervene if they learn that a four-year institution is treating transfer students differently from the way they treat their own native students. Program review powers are sometimes used to force articulation between related career programs, and funding incentives may be offered to encourage more cooperation. But there is a prevailing belief that articulation cannot be mandated, and most coordinating board officials appear reluctant to antagonize powerful four-year college and university interests by supporting community college efforts to reduce transfer barriers. While most state officials are not comfortable in talking about competition among public institutions, few will deny that such competition exists or that it can impede the progress of minority students.

Underlying all articulation issues is a continuing concern with the plight of the public schools in general and those serving urban minorities in particular. As one state official noted:

> Community colleges in taking on a special role in working with minorities have confronted an issue not unlike [that facing] the public schools. How do you focus on baccalaureate opportunities for a population for whom the lack of preparation and poverty make immediate employment their most urgent need?

State officials acknowledged that the graduates of some urban community college campuses were not the equivalent of those produced by suburban community colleges, but they were sympathetic to the problems such institutions faced. One state executive described the problems of high dropout rates and low reading levels in high schools and went on to note that "given the students they must work with, they may be doing more in terms of value added than most other institutions." He then added:

> The community college mission involves remedial responsibilities. This is a horrendous problem. Perhaps in the final analysis, a community decides where its students are best placed.

From the perspective of the staffs of coordinating agencies, articulation problems occur in part because community colleges "have tried to address so many things that articulation has not been a priority. They think universities will come to them." Unfortunately, the colleges and universities that do come to urban community colleges are not always the ones that could contribute the most to baccalaureate opportunities for placebound urban minority students.

General Strategies. Most coordinating agencies described themselves as reactive rather than proactive for the simple reason that advocacy of controversial issues posed a real threat not only to the agency's informal authority but also to its continuing viability. In one of the states with a strong coordinating board, the chief executive officer noted:

> This agency operates in a very fine gray area. There is always a bill sitting somewhere to do away with us. We are criticized by institutions for not taking more of an advocacy role, but the legislature also criticizes us for being too institutionally oriented.

In most of the states in our study, relationships between coordinating agencies and institutions were fairly cordial; in two states, however, the coordinating board had lost important battles within the past two years. In one instance, an attempt had been made to force two institutions to merge, while in the other officials had attempted to close a program at one of the stronger universities. Coordinating board staff in these agencies felt that their position had been seriously affected by these incidents and that any subsequent confrontations of similar magnitude in the near future would be catastrophic.

In states, such as the two described above, where relationships between coordinating agencies and institutions were less cordial or even openly antagonistic, state agencies seemed to spend more time preaching at institutions and less time developing institutional consensus about the need to address key issues. These states did not have well-developed data bases and relied heavily on legislative relationships and political advocacy. Legislative advocacy is, of course, an important responsibility of coordinating boards in all states. Those that have the best relationships with educational institutions in the state are those that consult with them about issues before taking a legislative stance. It is easier for university administrators to accept a coordinating board position unfavorable to institutional interests if there is prior understanding of the nature of the disagreement and of the data used in the decision process.

Coordinating boards devote most of their time and energy to four-year colleges and universities. While this emphasis is a natural consequence of differences in status as well as of the greater state responsibility for the funding and governance of four-year institutions, in several states the relationship with community colleges approached one of benign neglect. In all the states, this arrangement translated into a reluctance to actively support the interests of the community colleges when such interests were in opposition to those of the universities. The reactive posture of coordinating agencies, along with their reluctance to be caught in the middle of conflicts between competing institutions, restricted their role in articulation to serving as a voice for executive or legislative interests and to acting as a convening authority for representatives from involved institutions. Community college administrators frequently called for a more active role for coordinating agencies in promoting course transfer and course acceptance, but this did not seem to be a realistic expectation.

Needless to say, the key to achieving state priorities is power, but few statewide boards have the authority to govern. Even when they do, community colleges generally are not included within their sphere of responsibility. But coordinating boards do use program approval powers as a means of eliciting desired responses from a college or university. In one state, approval of any proposed program submitted by a public four-year institution followed several screenings. These screenings began with a determination of the impact of the program upon nearby institutions, including community colleges. In several instances, boards required baccalaureate institutions to accept complementary community college programs as part of a two-plus-two transfer—a transfer arrangement whereby students completing a prescribed lower-division sequence were guaranteed a bachelor's degree after two additional academic years.

Several other strategies were in common use. One strategy involved highlighting problems or issues in an effort to build consensus about the need for action before undertaking a search for alternatives to current practice. Task force groups made up of key institutional representatives were formed to delineate and analyze problems, especially in areas requiring interinstitutional cooperation. Even when changes in practice did not follow such analysis, positive results were reported in terms of improvement in the level of communication and understanding between institutions. Another strategy reported was the use of external pressures to stimulate institutional response. One state official commented, "We have used the desegregation decree to get the attention of the universities, particularly after the legislature called for concerted efforts by all institutions." In another state, the governor gave priority to improving the quality of higher education, and this fact was used to exert pressure for change.

Still another strategy involved the use of public disclosure and the power implicit in information. A coordinating agency had been able to get the cooperation of all but two universities in assembling data requested by the legislature. In previous years, the agency had attempted to cover up for the recalcitrant institutions in the hope of encouraging future cooperation. "This time, however, we inserted in bold print at the beginning of our report the fact that it was incomplete because information had not been given by X and Y universities." The official then observed that the last two requests for information had not only been honored by these institutions but that data from them were among the first to be received by the agency. Yet another coordinating agency published a list of admission criteria for each of its public universities as a technique for spotlighting that several institutions continued to maintain low admission standards, despite legislative demands that requirements be tightened.

Coordinating boards also attempted to persuade legislatures to provide categorical aid to encourage institutions to focus on state priorities. Typically, these efforts focused on selective excellence and increasing the number of minorities enrolled. Funding strategies were also used as disincentives. In a state that had established enrollment caps for lower-division students within the university system, reports of violations resulted in a funding formula change that cut off additional funds when the caps were exceeded. The impact of these strategies is revealed in the discussion of coordinating board operations that follows.

Coordinating Board Operations

Coordinating boards exercise their influence on urban higher education primarily through the manner in which they implement the core functions of planning, budget review, and program review. In terms of minority student achievement, the first two are more important than the third. In addition to core functions, coordinating boards also affect higher education opportunities for minority students through data collection and reporting, assessment programs, and financial aid policies. Each of these major areas of state influence is considered more fully below.

Planning. The level and sophistication of planning activities varied widely from state to state. On one end of the continuum were those states that operated primarily in a political mode and simply formulated responses to threats or opportunities as these appeared in the state environment. On the other end, coordinating agencies used well-developed strategic planning procedures "to raise issues among ourselves before someone outside does so."

Planning as it is practiced in the 1980s differs markedly from the kind of planning typically done by states in the sixties and seventies. Five-year master plans were conspicuous by their absence. As one state official noted:

> We found the cost-benefit ratio for long-range planning to be unfavorable in the current environment. In addition, we were uncomfortable in forcing institutions to plan within predetermined categories as we did when master planning during the seventies.

Instead of working out elaborate documents that will eventually gather dust on office shelves, planners now attempt to identify and deal with selected issues that have the greatest priority or are most critical for the state.

While this approach resembles strategic planning, it is not as formalized or extensive as the latter. In our sample, the planning process typically began with the identification of key issues through the use of data-based studies, development of position papers authored by staff, or the use of broad-based task forces that focused on areas of general public concern. Issues were sometimes identified by the legislature or the executive branch, but in other instances they surfaced through staff dialogue supplemented by consultation with advisory committees composed of college and university staff.

The states involved in more sophisticated planning processes had strong data bases. Those not involved in systematic planning had very limited information and even less capability for collecting data in response to issues or questions raised by concerned policymakers. Thus, in a state with a strong planning process, the chancellor described the purpose of planning as "raising issues of the relationship between what an institution does and the larger concerns of society." Beyond pressing institutions to define their missions so as to avoid unnecessary duplication, the coordinating agency was attempting to convince the legislature to use additional funds as a means of encouraging institutions to strengthen high-quality programs rather than distributing additional appropriations equally over all programs.

In a nonplanning state where the budget was described as the "chief policy instrument," one major concern was how to get out of the trap of justifying increases in legislative appropriations on the basis of inflation and enrollment. In this state, a lower level of inflation combined with declining enrollments in many of the institutions had caused legislators to raise questions about whether funding should remain level or decrease as a result of this decline.

Budget Review. State coordinating boards exercised authority over the resource allocation process primarily by recommending categorical funding programs and by influencing the development of the formulas used to justify budget requests and to distribute funds after legislative appropriation. Most states had developed alternatives to funding universities and community colleges on a strict credit hour basis. In the larger states, formulas included differentials based on unit cost analysis either at the program or the course level. But the results of such formulas were not always those anticipated. In response to the generally higher level of reimbursement provided for vocational/technical courses, one urban college had classified as many of its courses as possible in this category, including accounting, computer science, and even psychology courses. Administrators willingly traded transfer possibilities for increased state revenues.

State funding policies had an impact on minority student opportunities primarily through provisions for funding remedial courses and support services. In extreme cases, universities were excluded from state reimbursement for the student credit hours generated by remedial courses. More typical, however, was a limit on the number of remedial courses for which state reimbursement was provided to six to nine semester hours in mathematics, English, and reading. Universities received funds for support services primarily through categorical grants. Services beyond those supported through such grants were funded out of general university appropriations. Most universities were reluctant to aid underprepared students with funds that could otherwise have been applied toward the support of research.

While community colleges had fewer budget restrictions in offering remedial courses and support services, they encountered a different problem. Remedial courses typically were funded at levels lower than or equal to those established for college-level students in related disciplines. As a result, the smaller classes required for effective remedial instruction could be offered only by increasing class sizes for the prepared students, and special support services for minority students had to come out of the same revenue sources that funded all other expenditures. Community colleges were more committed to providing the support services needed by the minority and underprepared students than were their university counterparts; however, they frequently had less in the way of available resources. While some states had a special funding category for developmental or remedial courses, none had yet faced up to the true costs of providing the services required to assist remedial students without limiting the opportunities for well-prepared students.

In instances where state-level coordinating agencies had not identified minority achievement as a priority and structured incentives to encourage institutional response, strategies seemed less focused and more tentative. In one state, the board of trustees for the university system was struggling with the question of whether to establish a special systemwide fund to promote minority student achievement. In this same system, the practice during the past several years has been to avoid the redistribution of funds among universities by treating all of them equally in terms of increments or decrements to the base budget. This practice has operated to the disadvantage of the less mature urban institutions within the state system. The stress on commonalities and equal treatment in budget allocation procedures presented a marked contrast to the emphasis in other states on unique strengths or selective excellence.

Program Review. This function influenced minority student achievement in indirect ways. Several boards used the approval of new baccalaureate programs as a means of encouraging universities to pay more attention to articulation with community college career-oriented programs in such areas as nursing and computer science. While such pressure caused considerable resentment among university administrators, the outcomes appeared to be beneficial for students attending community colleges. At the same time, the demographic and fiscal conditions that prevail in a number of states have caused coordinating boards to be cautious about approving new degree programs. The consequences of this hesitancy have fallen most heavily on urban universities. Such institutions often are newer and have fewer programs than their better established flagship counterparts. When programs are unavailable at an urban university, students must transfer or relinquish career objectives. Moreover, the transfer process causes more difficulties for minority students than for nonminority students because of the high proportion of the former who are economically or educationally disadvantaged.

Data Collection. States with the most sophisticated planning activity have the best information systems. Their less sophisticated counterparts relied on the federal Higher Education General Information Survey (now IPEDS) as their major data base. Typically, their analytical capacity was limited. Most of their information derived from ad hoc data collecting. The only information available on minorities in one state was from institutional reports collected as part of the requirements of a desegregation plan. Perhaps more critical was the limited use made of available information to raise issues or questions about the direction and priorities of the system.

One state had developed an information system for articulation between community colleges and universities in response to a legislative mandate that called for statewide monitoring of transfers. Other states had developed or were developing unit record systems to provide data on all students in the two-year and four-year college systems. However, the state with the longest experience with such a system did not use it to provide institution-specific data on the progress of transfers by major or by associate degree completers or noncompleters. While this state had recently completed a pilot study of articulation practices between community colleges and state colleges and the outcomes of these practices, the study did not disaggregate results by race, nor was the research university system included.

Assessment Programs. State coordinating agencies increasingly are assuming responsibilities for administering assessment programs either by legislative mandate or by policy of the coordinating board. Two of the states in our study required a basic skills test for all prospective freshmen; only those who demonstrated a prescribed proficiency were permitted to enroll in college-level courses. Those who did not meet minimum standards were not permitted to register for regular academic courses in the areas where they were deficient. Colleges were required to place students with deficiencies in remedial courses that carried no college credit but did keep students eligible for financial aid. Both states have provided categorical funding to support these programs but have placed a limit on the number of remedial courses that can be taken. In one of the states, students who score in the lowest quartile (equivalent to scoring below the sixth-grade level) are required to participate in adult basic education programs of public school districts before becoming eligible for community college remediation programs.

In two of the states, the coordinating agency was responsible for statewide assessment programs intended to measure the performance level of students enrolled in lower-division college work. In one, all sophomores attending the public community colleges and universities were required to complete all four subtests of an assessment battery before becoming eligible to receive an academic associate degree; however, successful completion of three of the four subtests permitted a student to transfer to a state university and a native student to continue in the upper division with the requirement that a passing score for the remaining subtest be achieved before the student registered for the thirty-seventh hour of upper-division course work. Several universities in other states have adopted their own assessment tests that they administer to native students as well as to transfers to avoid conflict with community colleges and the coordinating board. The results of these examinations were used only by the administering university. The state coordinating board did not have access to the information unless it was furnished voluntarily by the university.

Whether state or institution sponsored, assessment programs often were criticized as unjust or discriminatory in the case of minorities. Several strategies have been used to deflect this criticism. Typically, assessment programs were initiated over an extended period of time with the goal of sensitizing and conditioning students to the performance indicators required to progress in the system. Trial runs, in addition to conditioning students, offered opportunities for improving the validity and reliability of the programs. A second strategy used to counter criticisms involved setting cutoff scores at very low levels during the initial years of a program and then gradually raising them. In one state, the cutoff score for the performance test required of college sophomores was set as low as the ninth-grade level. Coordinating board officials estimated that it would be three years before the score would be moved to an appropriate level. This would permit those already enrolled to complete their degrees, while giving those about to enter the university advance warning about the requirements ahead.

State officials and institutional representatives were in agreement that assessment programs were raising academic standards for achievement, as reflected in an upward trend in test scores. There was similar agreement that minorities as a group had been adversely affected by these programs because of their initial lower scores. Despite this assessment, officials were optimistic because minorities have consistently shown gains in test scores for each year that the programs have been in operation.

Financial Aid

The policies followed by most state programs for administering student financial aid attempted to seek some balance between access and choice. Policies aimed at access target funds on low-income students and offer awards for both full- and part-time students. Policies aimed at choice restrict grants to full-time students and use total need rather than student income as the basis for making awards when the number of eligible students exceeds the dollars available.

In virtually all state-administered grant programs of major significance, most of the dollars flow to students attending private institutions. In cases where states attempted to balance their emphasis on access and choice, the proportion of dollars received by students at private colleges was as low as 60 percent. In states where the priority was clearly on reducing differentials between the costs of attending public and private institutions, thc comparable figures were as high as 80 percent. In the latter states, few or no grants were received by students attending low-tuition community colleges.

State financial aid practices in several states appeared to discriminate against transfer students. In a state where community college students were ineligible for state grants, transfers to more expensive four-year colleges and universities who became eligible for a state grant were classified as new students in the state's priority system, which gave preference to renewals. In the last year for which information was available for this state, the program ran out of funds for students with a documented need of less than $4,600.

The decision to promote access by extending eligibility to part-time students had the effect of reducing average awards to full-time students in the state with the best balance between access and choice. The level of funding approved by the legislature required that state awards be limited to 44 percent of tuition and fees. The priority system for awarding funds also made it unlikely that community college students who became eligible for a state grant through a midyear transfer to a more expensive four-year college or university would receive a state grant that year. By contrast, in another state where grants were limited to full-time students, the amount of a grant was refigured after a student transferred, and students were awarded any additional dollars to which they had become entitled. The latter policy seemed better calculated to enhance the achievement of urban minority students in baccalaureate programs.

The form required for students applying for state aid also impacts on minority students who begin baccalaureate study in a community college. Because students attending community colleges in several states either did not qualify for a state grant or were eligible only for very small awards, they typically used the no-fee federal form in applying for a Pell grant in preference to the American College Testing (ACT) or College Scholarship Service (CSS) forms, both of which involve a fee and are administered in conjunction with testing programs in which urban minority students rarely participate. States with poorly developed analytical capabilities required the ACT or CSS forms to cut down on their own paperwork. The effect, however, was to impose an additional hurdle between transfer students and the support they needed to maintain themselves in a four-year institution.

During the Reagan administration, those parts of Pell grants awarded for living expenses were applied to reduce eligibility for Aid to Families with Dependent Children. The award of Pell grants may also have an impact on eligibility for food stamps. While the rationale for these changes is clear, their impact has been to reduce the number of inner-city students living at or below poverty levels who can afford to attend postsecondary institutions. These policies may well account for a significant part of the decline in enrollment experienced by many inner-city community colleges that serve predominantly minority student populations.

Scholarships for minority students had been established in several states, most commonly as part of desegregation plans rather than as a special aspect of a state's financial aid program. The practice of preserving access through tuition subsidy seems to be in general retreat because of the impact of federal programs on tuition charges. However, one state has attempted to preserve at least part of the practice by requiring institutions to set aside a percentage of their tuition revenues for student assistance. A number of community colleges in the state have developed the practice of saving such funds and then requesting permission from the legislature to use them for constructing buildings. In justifying such a request, one president indicated that there were no needy students in his district. To encourage the use of these funds for the purpose for which they were intended, legislation has been adopted limiting the accumulation of such funds to 150 percent of one year's allocation.

There is considerable variation among states in the financial aid strategies that they have adopted for dealing with policy issues related to access and choice. Several are feeling a pinch because eligibility for financial aid has expanded more rapidly than have appropriations. All were concerned about the availability of federal funds, and several reported providing financial aid packages below the level of demonstrated student need. The most promising practices for improving minority student achievement included: accepting the no-fee federal form in addition to the ACT and CSS forms, making prompt award of financial aid entitlements resulting from student transfers to more expensive institutions, and increasing the number of semesters during which students who enter underprepared remain eligible for financial aid.

Conclusion

In all the states studied, minorities represented the fastest growing part of the student population, and in some of the states it was anticipated that they would represent more than half the student population by the year 2000. Together, urban community colleges and urban universities accommodated a larger proportion of the state's total enrollment of minority students than all the other institutions combined.

In a number of states, urban institutions have experienced significant enrollment declines. These declines have affected community colleges more severely than they have universities. The proportion of black students in attendance at urban universities has declined steadily over the last three to five years because of changes in admission requirements and reduced availability of financial support. These enrollment declines, especially among black males, threaten the achievement of equal opportunity goals and are a growing source of concern among policymakers at all levels of state government.

State coordinating boards influence institutional priorities by providing incentives for institutions to define areas of strength and to further improve programs in which they already excel. Incentives or penalties also discourage the pursuit of growth as an end in itself. When supported by a strong data base, the planning and resource process is used by many coordinating boards as a tool to encourage mission differentiation and to limit competition among institutions. Improving opportunities for minority student achievement requires, above all, institutional cooperation and the willingness to place state priorities for education above institutional interests. In an ideal world, leaders would keep the interests of their institutions subordinate to the public good. In the real world, motivating institutions to respond to educational needs from a system perspective requires determined and effective leadership from state coordinating boards

6

What Community College Students Expect from Higher Education

The primary point of entry to postsecondary education for urban students is the community college. According to Astin (1982), however, initial enrollment in a community college reduces the chances that a student will actually achieve the baccalaureate degree. Yet several studies suggest that the aspirations of minority students in terms of degree achievement are very similar to those of their nonminority counterparts (Center for the Study of Community Colleges, 1985; College Entrance Examination Board, 1985). The purpose of the present chapter is to explore some of the reasons for this gap between aspirations and achievement by comparing urban community college students with their more traditional full-time counterparts. We consider first the views of those who teach in and administer urban community colleges and follow this with a discussion of essays written by students that describe their home environments, their reasons for attending community colleges, and their future goals.

Community College Perceptions of Urban Students

The characteristics of students attending urban colleges reflect the demographic changes of the 1980s. They are less well prepared than their predecessors and more likely to be members of a minority group. Growing numbers of international students and recent immigrants, both legal and otherwise, swell English as a second language offerings. Of course, in the midst of these changes, some characteristics remain the same. Most students have jobs and family responsibilities, and many of them are first-generation college students. Some come to a community college because "it is warm and dry" or for financial aid, but the dominant theme is that of students who are making their last try for formal education. There is a sense of urgency about the need to be productive and to improve themselves.

According to faculty and administrators, fewer students than in the past are interested in earning baccalaureate degrees and more want to obtain job skills for immediate employment. But common understandings can be deceptive. Colleges do not know why students attend them except in very general terms. Perhaps this reflects the level of indecision and ambiguity among students themselves. Colleges do know which courses students are enrolled in for reimbursement purposes, but most have little reliable information on such critical issues as the number of students who plan to transfer or their academic majors. The information that is available frequently is contaminated by an undecided classification that includes up to one-fourth or more of the total student enrollment.

Faculty and counselors were asked for estimates of student intentions. Such estimates were surprisingly consistent across the colleges. From 40 to 50 percent of the entering students were reported to have transfer as a primary objective. This estimate is very close to the results reported from a national survey of urban community colleges enrolling a significant number of minority students (Center for the Study of Community Colleges, 1985). The estimates of the number who might actually reach this objective in terms of behaviors ranged from 7 to 20 percent, which was not far from the 12 to 24 percent estimate of the survey mentioned above.

Students want to enroll in courses that will transfer even if their immediate objective is to gain employment. While this phenomenon frustrated faculty and counselors who had the responsibility for reconciling such conflicting expectations, they understood and sympathized with student reasoning. Many of those who attend urban community colleges are very poor. They need to support themselves and to contribute to the support of their families as soon as possible. But such necessity coexists with long-range aspirations to return to school and earn a degree that will confer professional status and open doors. Naturally, these students want to apply as many credits as possible from their short-term, career-oriented programs toward their long-term goal of earning a baccalaureate degree. The surprise is not that many fall short but that some persist against all odds and achieve the baccalaureate degree.

Community college faculty members differ in their perceptions of the needs of urban students. One view was illustrated by faculty at a predominantly minority campus who stated that their students should not pursue baccalaureate programs but should instead prepare themselves for employment. They argued that extreme poverty as well as the "obstacles of the system" made it unrealistic for students to dedicate years of time and energy to a goal seldom realized. At other predominantly minority institutions, however, faculty members and administrators were critical of those too ready to emphasize students' liabilities rather than their potential. On these campuses an array of motivational and support strategies encouraged minority students to raise their sights and to include the baccalaureate as a major option.

Assessment of the level of their academic preparation as a basis for placing new students in course work is another important source of information about students. However, in many urban colleges, less than half the entering students are assessed. In urban colleges where students are assessed, more than 90 percent may require remedial English, with somewhat fewer needing remedial math. Clearly such students confront major obstacles in the pursuit of other than low-level vocational offerings.

Table 3 summarizes differences between the majority of students who attend urban community colleges and those who attend residential four-year institutions. While full-time students in the traditional age range are present as a substantial minority in urban community colleges, their previous academic preparation limits their ability to undertake baccalaureate work without massive remediation. And the fact that most students are interested in becoming employed as soon as possible provides justification for the heavy emphasis that these institutions place on vocational offerings. We return to the question of student preparation and aspirations in Chapter Nine.

Table 3. A Comparison of Traditional and Nontraditional Students.

Traditional	*Nontraditional*
Full-time	Part-time/intermittent
Eighteen to twenty-two years old	Twenty-eight to twenty-nine years old
Residential	Commuter
Middle to higher socioeconomic status	Low to middle socioeconomic status
Parent high school and/or college background	Parent grade school/high school background
Print/reading background	Visual/oral background
Standard English	Dialectical English
Time organized	Poor time concept
Academic objectives	Occupational objectives
Minimally prepared	Underprepared

Student Essays

Autobiographical essays were used to gain glimpses into the lives of students attending the urban community colleges that we visited during the study. The students who wrote essays were selected by faculty from English classes whose racial composition generally paralleled that of the institution. Each student was asked to address three broad questions in the writing assignment: (1) family background, work, home life, obligations, and problems; (2) reasons for attending a community college; (3) future aspirations and ultimate career and education goals. Many of the essays were written as part of a normal ungraded assignment administered on the first day of the semester to check placement in English classes. The diversity of those responding is reflected in the following sketches:

> Annette, the second of seven children of a Louisiana rice farmer, was attending college to earn a bachelor's degree in business administration while working full time as a laboratory assistant in a medical center to support her two teen-agers, the product of an unsuccessful marriage.
>
> Sarah, a fifty-eight-year-old black woman, who wrote that she was married when she was twenty and was still married to the same man, grew up in the South when high school was not a possibility because the $50 a month tuition that she would have had to pay to attend a boarding school (black children where she lived had access to public education only through the seventh grade) was more cash than her family saw in an entire year. Sarah completed high school in 1983 and planned to complete a B.A. degree.
>
> Thomas, a young black man, married with two children, planned to earn a baccalaureate degree in computer science, a field in which he already held a good job. Describing himself as "at first outraged" about writing an autobiography because "who really cares about an average black man's life," Thomas gave the assignment second thought and decided that since only rarely are "blacks offered a chance to put in writing, words about themselves," he would do it because "anything of importance in America is written down somewhere."

> Charles, a forty-five year old who was born in the former colony of British Guiana, was now working only part time, which left primary responsibility for supporting his three daughters and himself to his wife. His ultimate aspiration was the achievement of a Ph.D.
>
> Sam, a twenty-five year old, came from a family where there had been very little opportunity for education; his wife, in contrast, was the daughter of parents who were professionals. Sam's major objective, in addition to making a better life for his family, was to be able to "stay in the same room with my mother-in-law, carry on a conversation, and not be corrected." He wanted to help his wife have a better life "but most of all prove my wife's family *wrong.*" The emphasis was Sam's.
>
> George, who had grown up in the heart of the city as one of six children whose parents divorced before he finished grammar school, vividly described the effects of poverty. His mother, while not well educated, worked hard to keep the family fed and clothed. George began postsecondary education in a rural university but was forced to drop out for financial reasons. Now attending an urban community college while working full time as a clerk for the Social Security Administration, George hoped to transfer and ultimately complete the examination for certified public accountants.

These sketches could be duplicated almost at random from the nearly 800 essays submitted. Taken as a group, they present a compelling portrait of people who attend urban community colleges. One way of communicating the richness of their spirit and the demands of their environment is to let them speak in their own words.

City Environments. The students who attend urban community colleges can be described as low-income, underemployed or unemployed, single parents, older, immigrants, educationally disadvantaged, and so on. The reality of these terms is not communicated by the percentage figures that normally accompany them. Cities remain magnets for those seeking a new and better life, and community colleges occupy the front lines in the continuing effort to assimilate the divergent cultures that characterize American society as they do in no other place in the world.

The messages that the essays convey are as interesting for the questions they raise as for the ones they answer. Clearly, a majority of these students are women, and many are single parents, which reflects one reality of the urban community college clientele. The writer of the last passage below is of Asian ancestry, a fact that may or may not be evident from the content. Families are sources of inspiration as well as of discouragement. Some students are well prepared but most are not. The excerpts that follow suggest the range of backgrounds from which urban students derive their motivation and sustenance:

> My mother is unemployed. My mother, my three sisters, and I are living on food stamps and a check sent by the government monthly. The only problem that would keep me from completing my educational program is financial problems. For instance, I barely have enough money to pay for my textbooks and transportation to get to college every day.

> We moved from Mississippi in 1977, and I received the unique opportunity to attend a high school that was 75 percent white after attending grade schools that were 100 percent black. I looked upon the years at South High as some of my best and most productive. I excelled in physics and chemistry and joined the wrestling team and the chess team. At South I discovered the world. . . . Right now I am working to improve my grades and looking forward to transferring to a major four-year institution in early 1986.

I'm twenty-seven years of age and a single parent. Both of my parents were born and raised in the state of Arkansas. They didn't receive a high school education because they had to work and help take care of their younger sisters and brothers. They didn't have much schooling, but they read for us and made us read. My two oldest brothers didn't complete the twelfth grade. I dropped out of school at sixteen years old to become an instant wife and mother. At age twenty-one, I returned to school and received a GED after six months. I then entered a vocational school, which I completed in one year, and have since passed the state board exam. I have been working as a licensed practical nurse. I have not taken any college courses until now.

Since my husband makes just a little over minimum wage, and is the only one working right now, it gets a little difficult to concentrate on studies. We both agreed I would not work during my first two semesters so I could obtain the highest grade point average possible and so that I could get back in the swing of going to school full time again. . . . I didn't take high school very seriously, I guess. In the tenth grade, I decided to drop out, but soon I was dissatisfied with jobs only "dropouts" could work on, so I returned and obtained my GED. Later, I enrolled in a vocational/technical school and received a certificate which qualified me to work as a clerk-typist. Since then, I have taken self-improvement courses, attended seminars, and I am certified to work as a teacher's assistant.

I'm attending school this final year on a scholarship. I should not have been able to attend otherwise. My husband makes enough money to disqualify me for financial aid. Our debts are staggering after the years of child rearing. The scholarship is great and pays my class fees. I had a problem trying to get the money together for books and other materials. I thought I was going to have to withdraw. It seems that you have to have applied for financial aid to get a book loan, and that only would have helped me the first year if I had. What does the scholarship student do who cannot buy books? My books alone are about $87. I was fortunate in help from staff personnel in finding me work in their department. One instructor even loaned me the money to buy my books so that I wouldn't fall too far behind. I can't help thinking of the student in my situation who is struggling to support herself. The problem of buying books, even if tuition is free, can be a real hardship at this time of their life.

I'm presently living with my grandfather. He is providing me with a home while I work toward my A.A. degree. Our agreement was that I work for a year to save enough money and pay for my first-year tuition and fees, after which he would pay the rest. Having saved this money the past year, I have the advantage of not having to work presently, leaving all my time to my studies. My grandfather is sixty-four years old and is attending community college. This is his third year as a night student. Providing me with a home and financial help while in college is great, but seeing my grandfather go to college and enjoy his studies so much is an incredible inspiration to me.

It's been very hard to continue college because of my family discouraging me or financial problems. I initially started immediately after high school. But after heavy pressure from my family, who felt I was wasting my time, I dropped out during my second semester. I started working and finally, five years later, I am back! I hope I can support myself and complete my education.

> The background of my family is not really too much because my mother only finished the second year of high school, my father finished some college classes. . . . I'm starting my college education. My mother tells me to continue doing it, that I need that education and she wants to have a professional family because we are intelligent and we can do it. I came to this country four years ago and I finished high school so I better finish my education here because this is where I am living and will continue to live. One can have as good a future here as in any other country. The background of my family helps me to see how important it is to have an education so you can have a good future.

Student Goals. Two dominant themes appear in the following comments. First, there is the desire to qualify for a better job. Second, many seek guidance in setting career goals, which perhaps reflects the considerable disjuncture between their high aspirations and their meager preparation. Mixed in are some who are attending community college because they love learning as well as some whose career objectives require the baccalaureate. The range of responses, while predictable, shows infinite variation:

> I've always thought I wasn't college material, but I seem to be hanging in there. I enjoy learning because one day I will have to teach my son some of the things I have learned. I hope to get myself a job and make something out of myself.

> I am attending because one day I hope to have the better things life can offer. I feel education is the way to achieve those goals. Also, as I stated, I have an endless love for knowledge and books, and I have to learn all I can.

> After thirteen years of full commitment to my family and my children, I lost confidence and

felt that I was outdated. The community college provided me updated knowledge and the latest technology. Most of all, I regained my confidence. Now, I realize that I am still fit for the job market. I'm looking forward to a better life ahead of me.

I had never planned to attend a community college. I always planned on going directly to a four-year school, but things didn't quite work out as I had planned. When I was in high school I was a *C+* student. I could have done better, but I always procrastinated. That's just why I'm here. When I should have been filling out applications for colleges, I was probably out somewhere playing basketball.

I cannot decide what I really want as far as employment is concerned. So right now I'm taking general studies courses. I hope that community college will help me decide what career goals to aim for.

I am going to a community college because I am not quite sure of what field I want to enter. At the community college I think I can experience different kinds of areas and pick the one best suited to me. A community college is a good way to go through a lot of the lower-division classes because the classes are smaller and you receive more personal attention.

I attend community college because it is less expensive and I can also work. I like the atmosphere of my classroom but not the atmosphere of the student lounge and hallways. Some of the students act like elementary students. My teachers are great.

My reasons for attending community college are (1) to have a sense of worth, (2) to strive for knowledge, and (3) to prove to myself that I could do it. I had wanted to go back to school for several

> years but was afraid that if I did, I would end up being a failure. I was becoming so stagnant that I decided to see if I could cut it. I'm glad I did. I like the idea of being back in school. It is a whole new and different world.

> The reason I am attending community college is because I got an 820 on the SAT and the requirement of the university is 840. I have applied twice and have taken the stupid SAT test many times. I am an intelligent person who is very capable of going to college. It is really a frustrating thing to want to go away to college but can't because I am 20 points short of the requirement.

Looking to the Future. Some students have very specific objectives. Others are unsure of what they are seeking beyond the opportunity for a better life. Some federal and state policy officials may be uncertain about the returns of a higher education, but these students are not. Often attending at a considerable sacrifice to themselves or their families, they are determined to achieve through the community college their piece of the American dream. In a way they may be wiser than those who question the possibility of their succeeding. Education remains the last and best hope for urban students and especially for those who are immigrants or belong to minority groups. It is difficult to read the following comments without wanting to come to the aid of those who wrote them.

> After graduation I enlisted in the navy, where I served for four years. I was just recently honorably discharged. I decided it was time to get back to school, and so now I'm in my first semester. My major is dentistry. I'm planning to complete two years of predentistry and then to transfer and continue my education at a four-year university.

> I graduated from high school in 1981. I got tired of working jobs with no future. Jobs that

have you out of a job faster than you can start working. Now that I have a son, I feel I am obligated to provide him with the same type of upbringing I had.

I have always wanted to make something of myself, that I know for a fact. The sad thing is that I am not sure what it is. I figure I can get my basics out of the way and then maybe attend a four-year college somewhere. Sometimes I feel so smart and I try to set high standards for myself; then there are times when I feel so dumb and useless. I want to be something, so I figure college is where it is at.

My position at the company is a data-processing production coordinator. I have been with this company since January of 1978. After finishing my education here at community college, I want to become a manager in the data-processing field.

I feel that life for me will be very different because of a bachelor's degree, because it will allow me to get more than just a restaurant job.

College has become very important to me because without it, I will not be able to advance in my profession (law enforcement). Also, I won't be able to capitalize on money given for degrees. This would mean less, and less opportunities for me to get a better job. So I now have been forced to get my degrees, so I can open doors.

Presently, I am working as a social worker in the county jail. My dream is to be a lawyer. I would like to have my own office and be successful.

My major goal in life is to achieve my master's degree in management. After completing community college, I intend to go to a major university and achieve this goal.

> In 1979 I became ill again, but continued to work until 1981 when I found it necessary to quit both jobs. My life's ambition is to complete four years of college, majoring in computers, so that I can get a job within the scope of my physical capabilities so that I can become completely independent once more.

> The reason I go to college is because I come from a very poor family and I would like to make something of myself. I would like to be able to live like a half-normal family and I do like school so this would be the best for me.

> I would like to be able to become a doctor in the field of medicine, maybe with children.

> My hope and aspiration is to become an interpreter for the hearing impaired.

> I plan to become a physical therapist.

Emerging Themes

The intent of this chapter has been to describe the urban community college student as a person rather than simply treat him or her as a statistic. Many of the essays that the community college students wrote exhibited commonalities across the different cities in our study. In the remainder of the chapter, we discuss these commonalities, as well as report some differences between students from urban campuses and those from suburban campuses.

Use of the Community College. Two reasons for selecting community colleges were prominent in the essays. First, an overwhelming majority of the respondents indicated that they had turned to the community college because of its low cost. Financial need was again and again mentioned as a barrier to higher education. Further, a majority of the students worked either full time or part time while attending college. Some worked full time and attended part time, while others were able to reverse the pattern. But financial need was a dominant factor in their personal and educational lives. The second major reason for choosing a community college was proximity of the college to the student. This of course also relates to cost. Many indicated that the community college was convenient to their work, others that it was close to their homes. Proximity was always discussed from an economic perspective, not from a time or convenience perspective. So low cost and proximity remain, as they have been since the beginning of the community college, the dominant variables that influence student choice.

Most of those attending inner-city campuses, as distinct from those attending more suburban colleges, were the first in their families to seek a college education. High school graduation was typically the highest level of education attained by their parents, but it was not unusual for one or both parents to have terminated their formal schooling in the elementary or secondary grades.

A sizable number of students used the community college as a proving ground. Some were forced to do this because they had been high school dropouts and met entry requirements through completion of the GED, while others acknowledged that low achievement and poor grades were instrumental in their choice of the community college. The open-door policy and remedial/developmental programs became the key to access for them. Older community college students, both male and female, frequently reported that they had previously attended the community college where they were currently enrolled. Many had completed courses or programs that had permitted them to find employment. Now, while still employed, they were returning to the community college in order to prepare themselves for transfer to the university and for their ultimate goal of a baccalaureate degree. These essays give credence to the community college objective of providing students with entry-level skills for immediate employment, without requiring them to relinquish their long-term objective, the bachelor's degree.

Profile of the Students. The writers were generally oriented toward human service careers. Many expressed the desire to help others after achieving their own objectives. Large families were much in evidence. The median number of siblings reported was four, and the range extended at the high end to twenty-one. A picture of love and caring emerged, as well as one of zest for life. Many of the writers were able to see humor in their situations and typically were optimistic about the future. While many of the students were older, as might be expected from the comments previously reported, 79 percent were below the age of twenty-five, a finding that suggests that inner-city colleges have retained a larger share of the younger full-time students than their more suburban counterparts, perhaps because there are fewer alternatives available to these students. Forty-five percent of those writing essays were black, 8 percent were Hispanic. Two-thirds of all respondents were women. While the sample was one of convenience, the characteristics of those responding were not very different from those reported by Davila (1985), who included eight four-year institutions in her sample of ten institutions.

A large percentage of the essays exhibited naiveté about careers. It was obvious that many students functioned at a fantasy level in terms of their awareness of the demands of a hoped-for career. In identifying academic majors, students evidenced a lack of understanding of the prerequisites necessary to achieve desired goals. From these essays, it was clear that career counseling and advisement were essential support services that deserve the priority they have been given by most community colleges.

A positive attitude and appreciation for the community college and its faculty were evident in the essays. Older community college students expressed gratitude for educational opportunities that they once thought had permanently passed them by. College age students expressed satisfaction or appreciation for their college experience and for the interest and support of faculty and staff. Like older students, they also thought that the community college was making a difference in their lives. At the same time, many respondents expressed apprehension about attending a university, which they assumed would be an unfriendly and unsupportive place. They saw the need to "prepare first" at the community college. The few who were critical of the community college in their essays felt that they had been badly served by the system or by individuals within the college in areas such as registration, academic advisement, and financial aid.

Role of the Military. One theme that emerged from the essays was the underrepresentation of black males in postsecondary education. Nearly two-thirds of the essays were written by females, who often, however, described the educational and vocational activities of their brothers and sisters. There was a discernible pattern according to which male siblings entered military service immediately after high school. Those who went into detail in the essays invariably indicated that their siblings chose military service over education to learn skills or to receive training that would equip them for careers. Among the essay writers who were veterans, it was typical to credit the military for giving them a "way out" and opening up career opportunities. These writers provide evidence that many low-income high school students see military service as more desirable than education because of its more immediate payoff and because it opens career doors for them when they return to civilian life. Also interesting was the number of minority women who gave their goal as enlistment in a branch of the military. In most instances, entering military service after receiving a B.A. was seen as assuring the woman a commission as an officer. The perceptions and career aspirations of minority females thus seemed pitched at a different level than those of their male counterparts.

Suburban Versus Urban Backgrounds. Two of the community colleges from which essays were obtained were more suburban than inner-city institutions. The socioeconomic composition of these campuses was significantly more middle income and more white than that of the urban schools. Parents were more likely to have attended college, and many were college graduates. It was not unusual for both parents of a student to be professionals.

The essays written by the more suburban students seldom spoke of the neighborhoods in which they lived. Many of the inner-city students, in contrast, expressed special pride or satisfaction in living in "a clean, quiet neighborhood," as if such an environment was unusual among their peers. Others described their neighborhoods as "safe," and one writer commented, "In our neighborhood, we look out for each other." It would appear that suburban students can take for granted some of the living conditions that are noteworthy for many urban students.

Another striking contrast between urban and suburban students emerged from what appeared on the surface to be a common concern about financial matters. Though working full time or part time was a common pattern in both settings, it was clear that the urban students' financial situation was more precarious and that lack of financial aid or income from a job would bring an end to attendance at school. In contrast, most suburban students did not report the need to interrupt their education if they were unable to find work. Their parents could or would find a way for them to continue their education.

Like their more urban counterparts, suburban students did address indebtedness and economic concerns in their essays. A majority of the suburban students, however, described their financial responsibilities in terms of having to maintain a personal automobile and lamented the high cost of insurance; some implied that it was unfair for the system and/or their parents to expect them to carry such a burden. Many of the suburban students also said that they had to pay the community college tuition from their own income (even in cases where both parents were practicing professionals). In some families, the student reported having to pay tuition and personal clothing costs, while in others the student was responsible only for the cost of maintaining his or her automobile. Occasionally, students were required to make a weekly or monthly contribution to the family budget. But the financial burdens mentioned by suburban students, while real, represented different kinds of dilemmas than the survival issues confronting inner-city students.

Conclusion

Many provocative concepts emerged from the comments of the urban essay writers. Some spoke of the importance of education in "making it," while others spoke of education as "a way out." In some cases, such comments were found in papers that also spoke of a happy family life, a good neighborhood, and blessings from God. What is the meaning of the apparent contradiction here? This faith in education as a panacea would support the hypothesis that the writer was searching for something that he or she had not fully identified. As sociologists have observed, the educational system in America is built on middle-class values and traditions. To succeed in the system, one must understand these values and function accordingly.

The goals of many writers appeared unrealistic in the extreme. And yet, America is built on the unrealistic aspirations of generations of immigrants who somehow found ways to achieve those aspirations—to achieve them for their children if not for themselves. Whatever else one may conclude, it is not possible to write these students off as the product of a mistaken national emphasis on access to education. When one looks below the surface of test scores, economic uncertainty, and previous educational performance, one finds human beings who are striving to realize the American dream in the face of many barriers. Many will not achieve that dream, but some will. Moreover, it is the dream that is important, not the success ratio. The community college for many of these students truly represents America's last frontier.

7

How Transfer Students Evaluate Their Educational Experiences

In the previous chapter, we heard community college students describe their family backgrounds, present realities, and future aspirations in their own words. From their essays and the perceptions of those who worked closely with them, it was clear that differences in achievement were not a function of any fundamental differences in career objectives. To identify some of the variables that frustrate these aspirations, this chapter reports the results of a survey administered to students who transferred from urban community colleges to urban universities. In addition to providing an overview of students who made the transition between conflicting cultures in spite of underpreparation and economic hardship, we report evaluations of their previous educational experiences and their suggestions for improving the transfer process.

The Student Survey

To determine student views of the transfer process, a survey was mailed to randomly selected samples of students who were enrolled at each of the nine universities during the fall

1984 term after completing at least thirty hours of credit at a paired community college. The survey, a copy of which appears as the Appendix, consisted of twenty-four forced choice questions and one open-ended question that asked for suggestions for improving the transfer process. Each sample included 100 students or the total transfer population for institutions receiving fewer than 100 students from a paired community college. The overall return rate was 58 percent, which provided reasonable assurance that the response was representative.

Table 4 provides information on the proportional representation of blacks and Hispanics at various stages of the baccalaureate sequence among the institutions studied. In interpreting these data, the reader should bear in mind that they represent snapshots rather than longitudinal studies of specific cohorts. The proportions of students who graduated were derived from university reports based on all students enrolled rather than exclusively on transfers, while the other estimates came from the survey. As a result, the figures cannot really be compared. Nevertheless, they do convey a sense of the extent to which transfer students from urban community colleges represent a source for addressing imbalances between minority and non-

Table 4. Average Proportional Participation of Underrepresented Minority Students at Four Stages of the Process Leading to the Baccalaureate Degree.

	Proportional Participation		
Stage	*Black (percent)*	*Hispanic (percent)*	*White/Asian (percent)*
Enrollment in a community college	37	11	52
Graduation from a community college	32	8	60
Transfer to a university	33	9	58
Graduation from a university[a]	17	6	77

[a]The base for this proportion is not the same as for the other entries. See text.

minority graduation rates. The number of Native American students was so small in all institutions as to preclude reporting their experiences in a proportional analysis.

The rates of attrition for black and Hispanic students in the transfer process appear to be significantly lower than the comparable rates reported by universities in the study for lower-division attrition of black and Hispanic students who begin as native university freshmen. The implication that underprepared students who begin their postsecondary education in a community college may be aided rather than impeded in their pursuit of a baccalaureate degree needs to be treated with caution. The community colleges from which blacks were most likely to transfer at rates comparable to their representation in the overall student population were heavily or predominantly minority institutions. Even with this qualification, however, it is clear that urban community colleges deserve careful attention as potential contributors to any resolution of the disparities between minority and nonminority degree achievement.

Table 5 provides a breakout of the sample by racial group. On the average, black students were older than the other groups. A much higher percentage of black students were female, a phenomenon that has been widely noted, with justifiable concern. For the total group of transfers, females dominated all fields of study except for math, engineering, and the physical sciences, where traditional male dominance continued. Males and females were equally represented in computer science and business/accounting. Black students were overrepresented in allied health, education, and social sciences. They were most seriously underrepresented in mathematics, physical sciences, and engineering and related technologies. Hispanics were seriously underrepresented in fields requiring science and mathematics and generally were overrepresented in the same fields as blacks were. The fields chosen by blacks and Hispanics confirm concerns about their tendency to avoid career areas related to mathematics and the sciences. The underrepresentation of females in science-related fields appeared largely a phenomenon of the career choices of black females, who dominated their transfer cohort. Also of interest was the significant relationship

Table 5. Race, Gender, English-Speaking Background, and Age of Transfer Students.

					Percentage of Each Age Group			
Race	*(Number)*	*Percentage of Total*	*Majority Gender (percent)*	*Percentage Non-English Speaking When Growing Up*	*22 and Younger*	*23 to 35*	*36 to 45*	*46 and Over*
Asian/Pacific Islander	(31)	5	55 Male	81	29	65	6	0
Black/Afro-Americans	(178)	30	65 Female	6	15	53	21	11
Hispanic	(53)	9	55 Female	79	34	58	6	2
White	(308)	52	51 Female	7	29	55	10	6
Total[a]	(592)		55 Female	19	24	56	17	7

[a]Named categories do not include all respondents.

between growing up in a non-English speaking environment and the tendency to choose math- and science-related majors.

While conforming in general to the patterns noted above, there was diversity among community colleges in the choice of majors by transfer students. For example, among transfers from community colleges with black enrollments of more than 40 percent, the proportion of transfer students selecting majors in engineering and the hard sciences ranged from 7 to 26 percent. The institution that recorded the highest percentage of its students as entering science-related fields also had the most serious attrition of black students; blacks represented 57 percent of the community college's enrollment but only 32 percent among those transferring from the institution. The data suggested an inverse relationship between the emphasis placed on math and science by a community college and the probability that its black students would transfer. But the results also suggest that inner-city institutions can make choices about their curriculum and that such choices will be reflected in the career aspirations of their transfer students, including minorities.

The survey results confirm the role of urban community colleges as predominantly institutions for first-generation college students. Only in the case of Asian students had a majority of fathers progressed beyond high school graduation. Mothers were somewhat less educated than fathers for all groups. About 8 percent of the black respondents did not provide educational information on their fathers, reflecting perhaps the large number of single-parent black families headed by women. Asian fathers and mothers were the best educated. The percentages of parents holding bachelor's degrees or higher ranged from 8 percent for black fathers and 10 percent for black mothers, to 37 percent for Asian fathers and 33 percent for Asian mothers. Hispanic mothers and fathers also held more college degrees than did their black counterparts, but the differences were less dramatic than those between blacks and whites.

Table 6 compares the number of dependent children and hours worked by each of the groups. In line with national statistics on financial aid eligibility, black students were somewhat less likely to be employed, but the differences among groups

Table 6. Hours Worked and Dependent Children by Race.

	Hours Worked per Week			*Responsibility for Dependent Children*		
Race	*0 (percent)*	*Less than 20 (percent)*	*More than 20 (percent)*	*Total Percentage*	*Percentage Having 1 to 2 Children*	*Percentage Having 3 or More Children*
Asian	13	27	60	23	20	3
Black	20	9	89	42	33	10
Hispanic	15	4	77	17	17	0
White	16	12	70	22	19	4
Total	18	11	69	28	24	5

were small. Asian students reported less than half-time employment more frequently than did other groups. Overall, the relatively high percentages of students working half time or more was consistent with the prevailing picture of the urban transfer student as a part-time working person.

Significantly more black students reported responsibility for dependent children and were more likely to have larger families, again a finding that was not surprising. Hispanics were the least likely to have responsibility for dependent children, which reflected in part their age distribution. As noted previously, black students were significantly older than the other three groups. Examination of hours worked and number of dependent children by major and community college attended revealed some differences, but none that could not be explained by the differences in racial characteristics already noted.

All groups relied heavily on work and savings to finance their educations, as would be expected from the number who reported being employed half time or more. White students were significantly less likely to report eligibility for financial assistance, which was the second most important source of funds for the other three groups. Asians, whites, and Hispanics were much more likely to report assistance from parents or a spouse; this category was the second most important source of assistance for white students. Black students made up some of the difference in comparative absence of support from parents and spouses by their use of loans, with 30 percent indicating this as a very important source. Hispanic and white students made the least use of loans. Since these two groups were also the least likely to be eligible for financial assistance, they were substantially more dependent upon work and family support than were their counterpart groups. The differences in patterns of support for these students generally corresponded to the differences in family structure and socioeconomic status reported in the literature.

Evaluating Preparation for University Work. Transfer students were asked to report how they rated their preparation for university work by the schools and colleges that they had previously attended. We anticipated that minority students attending inner-city school systems would be more likely to find fault with their previous preparation than would nonminority students. The results failed to support this assumption. Black students were as positive as their white or Hispanic counterparts and sometimes even more so. Asian students reported that their strongest preparation was in math and science, areas in which other groups felt the least well prepared. An examination of the same information arrayed by community colleges indicated that students attending institutions that enrolled the largest proportions of minority students were the most positive about their public school preparation. With one exception, 10 percent or fewer of the students attending predominantly minority community colleges reported poor public school preparation. The one exception was the community college with the greatest discrepancy between percentages of minority students in attendance and those in the sample of transfer students. This same college transferred the highest percentage of students in math and science.

It seems likely that the satisfaction minority students reported with their public school preparation resulted in part from the fact that community colleges adjusted academic expectations to the preparation of the students that they received. The literature and our observations provide substantial evidence to support this hypothesis. At the same time, it may be that some urban students somehow succeed in obtaining better elementary and high school educations than the prevailing judgments about their systems would suggest are possible. Both hypotheses deserve further exploration.

The satisfaction with public school preparation for university work also held for preparation by community colleges. Because of differences in the way questions were worded, only the areas of reading and writing were directly comparable. Community colleges held a slight edge in writing while public schools were given better marks for preparation in reading, a finding that probably reflected differences in curricular emphasis. But the percentage of students who reported poor preparation in either setting was very small.

While blacks were the most positive about their public

school experience, Hispanics were the most positive about the community college, although differences between the two groups were for the most part small. Asians ranked their preparation in reading and writing at the community college significantly higher than in the public schools. Overall, whites and Asians were the most critical of their community college preparation; this judgment perhaps resulted from their greater propensity for entering math- and science-related fields, areas in which most urban community colleges do not seem to be strong. But in general all groups gave a decidedly positive endorsement to the preparation they received prior to entering the university.

A review of the same data arrayed by community college produced few surprises but some insight into the complexities involved in interpreting surveys. In one instance, two samples from the same predominantly minority community college were surveyed because the college sent a significant number of transfers to two different universities, one a research institution and the other a predominantly minority comprehensive university. While both samples were positive about their previous preparation, those attending the research university were much more critical of their community college preparation in every area except examinations. This observation again supports the notion that judgments about preparation are related in an important way to the expectations of the receiving institution. From these data it would be difficult to conclude that the differences in rigor and standards between community colleges and universities are as great as university faculty believe—at least in the upper-division classes that these students took.

Above-average ratings were received most consistently by community colleges enrolling the highest proportions of black and Hispanic students, a result that reflected the tendency for both of these groups to view their previous educational experiences in an extremely positive light. But in the aggregate, few urban students in the samples believed that their community college preparation had been anything other than very good or at least fair. Students were the most critical of their preparation in math and science.

The Transfer Experience. A series of questions solicited information about timing of the decision to transfer, elements influencing the transfer decision, use of community college and university resources in transferring, the match between community college and university courses, credits lost during transfer, and first-term success in the university.

As indicated in Table 7, black students, who on the average were older than members of other racial groups, were the last to decide about transferring. More than one in five decided to transfer after leaving the community college. Only 31 percent made that decision before arriving at a community college. In marked contrast, nearly one-half of the Hispanic and white students knew they were going on to the university before entering the community college. Asians resembled blacks in terms of the relatively small percentages of them who planned to transfer before attending a community college, but significantly more made their decision while in attendance at a college, leaving less than one in ten who made the decision after leaving.

Table 7. Timing of Decision to Transfer, by Race.

Race	*Before Community College (percent)*	*During Community College (percent)*	*After Community College (percent)*
Asian	32	55	10
Black	31	43	22
Hispanic	47	34	19
White	46	39	13
Total	40	41	16

Students who transferred in the areas of engineering, business, and mathematics were the most likely to have made early decisions and, somewhat surprisingly, so were social science majors. The higher the proportion of minority students attending a community college, the later were decisions to transfer, underscoring the importance of identifying potential transfer students early and providing them with sound advice.

The most important influences on a student's decision to transfer included the chosen university's available programs, its academic reputation, its proximity to the student's home, low tuition, and perceived relationship to career objectives (helpful in getting a job). Next in importance were the number of credit hours that the university would accept, advice of a friend, and family or job responsibilities. The pattern for all racial groups was essentially similar, but several variations were worth noting. White students were significantly less likely to be influenced by community college counselors and teachers or university representatives. This may reflect greater self-sufficiency, but, given very similar family backgrounds in terms of college experience, it seems more likely that the difference reflected the greater number of special programs at both community colleges and universities for which minority students were eligible.

An examination of the data by community college revealed wide variation among institutions. The number of students reporting that community college counselors and teachers were not an important influence on transfer ranged from 41 to 88 percent. With only minor exceptions, students gave almost identical responses for faculty and counselors. Put differently, if counselors were not important to the transfer decision in a college, neither were faculty. The pattern of these responses suggests the influence that institutional policies may have on student experiences. The community colleges in which counselors and faculty were most likely to be an important influence were those serving higher proportions of minority students and having minority leadership.

The survey also evaluated the usefulness of the resources that community colleges and universities provide to assist students in the transfer process. For all groups, the college catalogue was by far the most widely used and helpful source of assistance. Other resources used by more than half of the transfers included (in order of use): teachers, counselors, transfer guides, friends who transferred, and the registrar's office. Asian students were the most likely to use all these resources except for counselors and the registrar's office, which were used most frequently by Hispanics and blacks. White students were significantly less likely to make use of these various resources than were other groups.

Only 10 percent of the students found orientation sessions very useful, and 64 percent said either that they had not used them or that they did not find them useful. The rating for this service reflected as much as anything its absence in most community colleges. The ratings in general do not reflect a heavy emphasis within community colleges on helping students to transfer. Such help can be found by those who seek it, but the most common source is the college catalogue.

The pattern of responses to a similar question about the usefulness of university resources in the transfer process suggests that little systematic assistance was given. The most frequently used resources in order of use were the university catalogue, the admissions office, visits to the university, academic departments, and university publications other than the catalogue. Asians and blacks were the most likely to use university resources while whites were the least likely. The greater incidence of use reported by minority students for such services as visits to the university, orientation sessions, and special programs reflected the emphasis placed in many of the universities in our study on the recruitment of minority students, but the relatively small percentage of minority students reporting contact with a university representative (34 percent) reinforces impressions from the interview data that most students were required to negotiate the transfer process without much assistance other than what they could obtain from routinely available publications or offices serving the general public.

Sources of assistance provided by both community colleges and universities can be compared in terms of their usefulness to these students, although caution must be used in interpreting the results since the same resource may affect the transfer process in different ways. Community college faculty were consulted in the transfer process almost twice as often as university faculty were, and twice as many students found their assistance very useful. In contrast, university orientation sessions and catalogues were more frequently used and were more frequently rated as very useful than the same resources in community colleges. Community college financial aid offices were more frequently used and gave somewhat better satisfaction than did their university counterparts. Other differences in directly comparable forms of assistance appeared inconsequential.

Student responses to the survey confirmed observations made during the site visits. In universities that had developed special orientation sessions for transfers, more students reported using them and finding them valuable than did participants at universities where first-time students and transfers were served by a common session. Differences by field tended to reflect the racial distributions of transfer students majoring in those fields and were generally quite small.

Most of those in all four racial groups reported that the courses completed in their community colleges had been selected with a specific university degree in mind. Whites were the least likely to have done so and Asians the most likely. Among all groups, three out of every four indicated that their community college courses bore some relation to the degrees that they were pursuing at the university. From these responses it would appear that a disproportionate number of successful transfers pursued university degrees closely related to the courses that they took at a community college. The relationship seemed to hold even for groups that made late transfer decisions.

Table 8 provides information about the loss of credit during transfer. Overall, about four in ten students reported no loss of credit. But among those who did report loss of credit, the impact was felt disproportionately by blacks; thus, nearly three out of every four black students lost some credit. Even though white students were the most likely to report a difference between courses taken in the community college and university degree intentions, they were the least likely to report a loss of credit during transfer; almost half of them reported no loss. Those blacks who lost the most credit, as previously noted, were the last to decide about transfer.

A significant majority of all groups except Asians reported that they held the associate degree at the time of transfer; this is a somewhat surprising result given the lack of emphasis placed on the degree in several states and the tendency for community colleges to design their programs around the needs of part-time students not interested in earning degrees. The

Table 8. Degree Status, Class Standing, and Loss of Credit by Race.

Race	*Holding Associate Degree at Time of Transfer*	*Credit Loss During Transfer*			*Additional Loss: Credits Not Counted Toward the Baccalaureate Degree*			*Class Status*			
		No Loss	*1 to 10 Credits*	*Range of Loss*	*No Loss*	*1 to 10 Credits*	*Range of Loss*	*Fr.*	*So.*	*Jr.*	*Sr.*
Asian	32	35	21	3 to 40	69	14	3 to 23	0	19	48	29
Black	61	27	34	2 to 79	76	14	2 to 51	7	18	47	24
Hispanic	76	47	31	2 to 49	78	12	2 to 70	6	13	66	11
White	48	42	29	1 to 81	73	14	3 to 65	7	19	46	26
Total	54	42	29	1 to 81	75	14	2 to 70	6	18	48	24

Note: All figures in percentages.

lower percentage of Asians earning the associate degree can be explained by the fields they enter. It was rare for inner-city colleges to offer appropriate degree programs in engineering, math, and the sciences. Even where such programs were available, the small number of prepared students pursuing them frequently found that class schedules were inconvenient, and this encouraged them to transfer early.

The loss of credit in the second or departmental evaluation of the students' transcripts was much less of a problem for these respondents than suggested from the interview data previously reported. Still, one in every four students reported an additional loss of credit, with slightly higher losses among Asian students, who were least likely to earn associate degrees and hence more likely to have to undergo a credit-by-credit evaluation of their transcripts.

Only one student in four reported a class status below the junior level. This finding reflected both the number of students who transferred with degrees and the high-risk status of those who transferred without completing a substantial part of their lower-division work. A review of the data from Table 8 arrayed by participating community college revealed that the number reporting an earned associate degree varied according to the articulation policies of the state where a community college was located. In a state where formal policies emphasized the associate degree as a transfer credential, 98 percent of the students transferring from a community college held that degree. In another state where little or no emphasis was placed on the degree, 23 percent reported earning it.

Unfortunately, there appeared to be little relationship between holding the degree and loss of credits. In the state where 98 percent of the students transferred with the degree, 58 percent reported no loss of credit while in the state with 23 percent, 60 percent reported no loss of credit. The survey data corroborate and extend some of the information reported in the following chapter. In cities where the poorest relationships between universities and community colleges were observed during the site visits, three out of every four students reported some loss of credit. Among institutions where the best relationships between community colleges and universities were observed, the number was slightly more than one-half. However, these observations have to be qualified. For example, poor relationships were found in a state with exceptionally strong and formal articulation policies. But despite the pronounced differences between community colleges and universities, less than half the students reported loss of credit. So relationships between institutions were important but so were state policies, and the latter seemed able to compensate in some degree for an absence of the former.

As a final question bearing on the transfer process, we asked students to report the grades that they earned following transfer. The results appear in Table 9. More than three out of every four transfers reported passing all courses the first semester after transfer. Among the racial groups, Hispanics were the least likely to report passing all courses and whites the most likely, but the differences were relatively small. A majority of all groups reported that their community college performance was in the *B* range, with blacks significantly more likely to have been *C* students.

After transfer, blacks were the least likely to report earning lower grades in the university. The pattern for all racial groups was, however, essentially the same. A relatively small number of students, in no case more than 15 percent, reported an increased grade point average. A much higher percentage of each group, ranging from 33 to 42 percent, reported lower university grades. Asian students, who entered the science fields in disproportionate numbers, reported the greatest discrepancy between community college grades and those earned in the university. Blacks, who tended to enter nonscience fields disproportionately, reported the least discrepancy. The data, while self-reported, generally were consistent with the results expected from the literature and the unpublished studies of participating universities. The fact that black students reported the least loss of grade point average reflected their lower grades before transferring, the fields they entered, and the number who transferred to universities with a predominantly minority student body. Most interesting, however, are the similarities among all four

Table 9. Self-Reported Success After Transferring, by Race.

		Community College Grades			*University Grades Compared to Community College Grades*			
Race	*Passing All Credits First Term*	*A*	*B*	*C*	*Higher*	*Same*	*Lower*	*Term Incom-plete*
Asian	72	13	72	13	3	55	42	0
Black	70	14	55	28	15	45	33	4
Hispanic	67	19	62	19	6	51	36	8
White	78	29	54	16	10	43	40	5
Total	74	22	56	20	11	44	37	5

Note: All figures in percentages.

racial groups after transfer. Elsewhere, we have noted that minority transfer students do not perform in ways significantly different from other transfer students, an observation that these data support.

When the transfer process is examined in terms of the timing of the decision, influences on the student, course patterns, and loss of credit and performance, it becomes clear that there were variations among racial groups that did have an impact on the process. The tendency for black students to make later decisions influenced the number of credits they lost. But the more interesting variations were those produced by institutional practice and state policies. A majority of the students who responded to the survey reported that they had transferred without the benefit of direct contact with professionals from either their community college or the university. Loss of credit seemed more a function of state policies and institutional relationships than of race. Clearly, there are opportunities for institutional and state interventions that would improve effectiveness in this area.

Evaluating Instructors, Courses, and Services. A central theme of this report has been the ways in which the cultures of the community college and the university differ and the implications of those differences for institutional practice. It was our assumption that student perceptions of the environments of the two types of institutions would reflect these value differences. To address the question of differences in institutional practices and the implications of such differences, we asked transfer students to compare faculty members, course offerings, and support services in the community college where they began their education and in the university that they were currently attending.

A majority of the students saw no difference between community college and university faculty in terms of knowledge of subject matter and organization. Those perceiving differences along these dimensions gave the edge to university faculty. Differences were most pronounced for Asian students who majored predominantly in math- and science-related areas. Also interesting were the perceptions of black students, who were far more likely to see university instructors as superior on both these dimensions. Hispanic students, by contrast, were somewhat more likely to see community college instructors as better organized.

The community college has long prided itself on being a teaching institution. In our interviews, faculty members in community colleges often criticized such university practices as the use of graduate students to teach lower-division math and English courses. Overall for the 50 percent of the students who perceived a difference, two out of three thought that the community college teachers did a better job. But this edge in favor of community college teachers was a function of the perceptions of white and Hispanic students; blacks and Asians saw no significant differences between university and community college teachers. An examination of these same data arrayed by major field revealed that community college teaching in physical sciences, computer sciences, mathematics, and biological sciences held the widest margin over university teaching. Social science was the only field in which university faculty were seen as doing a better job of teaching. While institutional differences were generally inconclusive, the university whose faculty members held the widest margin over their community college counterparts in terms of better ratings of teaching practice was a predominantly minority comprehensive institution that emphasized its teaching mission.

Students reported the greatest differences between community college and university faculty in terms of openness to student ideas, availability, and helpfulness with career plans. In the first two areas, community college instructors held more than a three to one advantage, reflecting the supportive environment of the community college that we have described elsewhere in considerable detail. The results were much closer for helpfulness with career; this may have been a result of the greater concentration on the major that occurs in upper-division work. But even for this area, all groups except Asians found community college instructors more helpful. The patterns for all racial groups except Asians on the career question were very similar, which suggests that experiences with faculty members do not vary a great deal. Differences by institution and discipline revealed no interpretable trends.

Students were also asked to compare course offerings in

community colleges and universities along several dimensions. Community college courses were more likely to be offered at convenient hours and to be available in the major field. All groups except blacks found registration easier at the community college. The somewhat surprising edge given by black students to registration procedures in the university may reflect the emphasis on recruiting black students and the special provisions for registering them found in many of the universities. All groups except Asians gave community colleges their widest margin in the area of course availability, which reflected the community college orientation toward the part-time and evening student. This difference suggests one problem area for transfer students who must adjust to universities that remain oriented toward students who attend during the day. Asian students were the only group reporting greater convenience and availability in the university. This perception seems related to their tendency to major in math and hard science for which there were few advanced courses available in inner-city colleges.

In marked contrast to responses about convenience and availability, universities by a wide margin were reported to have courses more relevant to student goals and at more appropriate levels of difficulty. Of course, lower-division work emphasizes general education, while specialization occurs primarily during the junior and senior years. Our interview data corroborated the widespread faculty perceptions of greater rigor in university courses. Interestingly, many students also perceived a difference and by substantial margins endorsed the demands required by university courses. A substantial number of students, however, reported no difference in level of difficulty.

An examination of the data by community college revealed no consistent trends for inner-city colleges as distinct from their more suburban counterparts. The number of students reporting level of difficulty more appropriate at the university ranged from 26 percent to 73 percent. Of note, the low and high percentages were from the same community college and involved two samples of students, one that transferred to a predominantly minority, comprehensive university (26 percent), and the other to a research university (73 percent). Students attending the institution with the reputation for greater rigor were nearly three times as likely to report the level of difficulty as more appropriate in the university. Of the remaining community colleges where above-average proportions of students reported that university courses offered a more appropriate level of difficulty, two were inner-city colleges and enrolled high proportions of minority students, while the third was a predominantly suburban college with fewer than 20 percent minority students. There was a relationship between curricular emphasis in the community colleges and perceptions that university courses were at a more appropriate level of difficulty. Those institutions transferring higher proportions of students into engineering, math, and the sciences were the most likely to perceive university courses as having the more appropriate rigor.

Students were asked to compare support services in community colleges and universities along dimensions similar to those for academic offerings. In four areas students reported that universities provided better services than community colleges. Predictably, these areas included library facilities, social events, cultural events, and student centers. With very modest variations these differences were consistent for all racial groups. They were also consistent for all community colleges, although some clearly did a better job in these areas than others.

In three other areas—admissions, tutoring, and counseling—community colleges were given a slight edge, but the differences were not consistent across racial groups. Whites and Hispanics favored the services in community colleges, but Asians and blacks either perceived them to be better in the university or saw little difference. Looking at the same information by community college indicated that most of the students who reported that tutoring was better in the community college were concentrated in three institutions. In the remaining community colleges, students reported little difference or favored tutoring services in the university. A similar if not so dramatic distribution was characteristic of counseling services, with a preponderance of the votes that favored community colleges occurring in two institutions. But there was no overlap between the two sets of evaluations. That is, community colleges with the most strongly rated tutoring services were not the ones that received the highest marks on counseling services.

In most community colleges, students rated admission services better, but in four samples, the university admission services were rated as being better, sometimes by fairly startling margins: 49 percent to 9 percent in one instance and 55 percent to 18 percent in another. Again, there seemed to be no consistent patterns among institutions so that those community colleges given high ratings in one area did not necessarily receive them in others. In one instance, a community college that received strong ratings for counseling services was rated as having poorer admissions services than its adjacent university.

In two other service areas, orientation for new students and financial assistance, universities were reported as having better services overall but the differences were much less pronounced than for libraries, student centers, cultural opportunities, and social events. In the area of orientation, a significant number of students reported no basis for comparison. But among those students who did provide a rating, university orientation was the choice of all groups except Hispanics. The same general observation applied to financial assistance, although here the differences were much smaller and fewer students reported a basis for comparison.

The differences among community colleges on these two variables were worth noting. Despite the overall observations noted above, financial aid services were described as better than those at the university for one community college and equal in a second. In one of the two, student orientation was also perceived to be better, but this same institution was not among the stronger community colleges in terms of tutoring or counseling. It did get a very strong rating on admissions. But there appeared to be little if any correlation between the ratings received by different services at community colleges.

The information provided by students in evaluating faculty members, course work, and support services appears somewhat equivocal in terms of any conclusion that community colleges uniformly and systematically provide a more supportive environment than do universities. There was evidence that community college faculty members were more available to students and more open to their ideas. Community college scheduling practices seemed better attuned to the needs and schedules of part-time commuting students. Community colleges appeared more accommodating in admission practices and slightly more likely to provide tutoring services than universities. But most of the responses favoring community colleges in these areas were concentrated in a relatively small number of programs scattered almost randomly across the participating community colleges. Absent was evidence of any systematic, across-the-board emphasis to make environments more supportive for baccalaureate-oriented students. The comments reported in the next section of this chapter do suggest that community colleges are perceived to be more student oriented and more concerned about students as individuals.

Student Comments

The comments and advice students provided on the open-ended question that asked them to identify ways of improving the transfer process have been organized into four sections. In the first, comments reveal student perceptions of conflicting cultures. A second section reports comments and advice specific to community colleges, while a third provides the same information for universities. The final set of comments relates to system-level concerns that might most appropriately be addressed by state coordinating boards.

A Clash of Cultures? In Chapter Two we suggested that the community college and the university constitute different cultures that the student must negotiate in pursuit of a baccalaureate degree. Do students perceive this difference in cultures? The comments that follow leave little doubt about the issue:

> Make the academic standards a little more strict at a junior college. The professor should be a little more distant, not so understanding. The academic shock from a warm, caring junior college to a cold, impersonal university is somewhat over-

whelming. Junior colleges should not be a babysitting service for the community's elderly or youth. They should be up to university academic standards, which I personally don't feel they are. Too much pampering at a junior college.

In many situations, students from community colleges are reluctant to attend the four-year institution simply because of the stigma associated with community colleges. They fear they are not prepared. I feel the four-year university should make an overt attempt to recruit students from neighboring community colleges with the same zest used to recruit incoming freshmen. The four-year university should embrace the efforts of the community college and not belittle the product it produces.

Overall, the community college courses were greatly superior to the university courses because of the individual attention and help received, and the superior quality of the teachers at the community college level. Community college teachers are there to teach. The university teachers are there to do research instead of teaching.

I would like to see more personal attention given at the university like I received at the community college. Some professors at the university are not willing to teach. They are willing to tell people what they know. Half of my chemistry lecture class failed. That would never have happened at my community college.

I was dismissed when I first transferred because I tried to do too much too soon. The community college stressed helping the student while the university leaves students on their own to sink or swim. They were two different worlds. The university does not give as much consideration to working students with families and other responsibilities.

Advice to Community Colleges. Students treated universities and community colleges with a fairly even hand in recommending improvements. The largest single category of recommended improvements for community colleges focused on counselors. The following comments were typical:

> Counselors at the community college didn't know which of their courses would transfer to the university. They and the community college catalogue must stress the importance of talking with a university counselor or working with universities in helping with the selection of transferable courses. Many community college students are not aware that some of their courses won't transfer.

> Everything is working fine except for the credit hours at the community college; most of them are not transferable. I think the counselors at the community college should be aware of all the courses that are transferable and give the students more information about other universities, as well.

> I would suggest that both the community college and the university hire more counselors and train the ones they have better. One counselor says one thing, admissions says something else, and teachers will say something completely different. Sometimes I think they are after my money instead of helping with my education.

> Community colleges need to expand their counseling services and place additional emphasis on identifying specific skills and interests of new students. The young students I encountered knew little about their true interests, were confused about their values, and were easily attracted to

> glamorous "get through fast programs," thereby wasting precious time and money when those areas could easily have been identified by a competent counselor administering a variety of tests.

A second area that received substantial emphasis in student comments involved the need for orientation and early information:

> Transfer students should have at their disposal easy access to major university requirements, transfer procedures, and a list of what courses the university will accept or reject.
>
> Community college counselors should encourage incoming students to consider whether courses will or will not transfer even if the student does not intend to transfer at that time.
>
> I would suggest a type of orientation at the community college where they explain the financial resources available and courses a student should take to prepare for the university. The university was much more difficult than the community college for me and I was not adequately prepared for the transition.

There were many comments on academic procedures, course availability, and course rigor:

> I was allowed to register for advanced classes regardless of course prerequisites.
>
> Core courses should be taken at the university. Community colleges don't have the perspective of the continuity of core classes.
>
> Community colleges should better prepare their students for longer and more complex reading assignments. The exams should be more diffi-

> cult, and they should be structured for testing a student's knowledge of the material instead of simply memorization and recall.
>
> Course work, especially in the field of mathematics, should be more demanding. Too many teachers compromise the standards on tests. At the university the tests are harder. . . . The community college atmosphere lends itself to that of a high school. Standards should be raised to prepare the student for the challenge yet to come.
>
> Place more emphasis on reading, writing, and mathematics skills at the community college level.

Advice to Universities. Universities received many suggestions for improvement but few accolades for current practice. Advice to the university contrasted sharply with advice to the community college, which was heavily interspersed with positive comments and a sense of appreciation. Students perceived many of the same problems with the university response to transfer students as were reported by administrators in universities and administrators and faculty in community colleges. Some of the advice focusing on the transfer process itself follows:

> Transfer students need orientation and tours of the facility as much as freshmen. The buildings could be better marked. Also, more maps and arrows would be helpful. This university is very spread out and interwoven with businesses, office buildings, and shops, which are not a part of the university.
>
> I strongly suggest that universities show a stronger representation on community college campuses.
>
> There should be some way of visiting a class in a university to see and know what to expect from a university before you enter.

> The university should give the student a chance to preregister for classes. Residual and late registration are very hectic and can turn a student off to college immediately.
>
> I wish they would evaluate the transfers faster. I had to take courses over because I didn't know if they would transfer. I lost a lot of hours and this set me back a semester.

A second predominant theme in student comments focusing on the university had to do with courtesy and university attitudes:

> Improve the attitude of employees and change the attitude of instructors. This university caters to the young students who are supported by their parents and live on campus. The constant comment I hear is: "Come back tomorrow." It is a thirty-mile drive for me. The transfer from the small-town atmosphere of a community college to this metropolis is horrifying. The cold atmosphere and feeling as though one is no more than a number (and any assistance is troublesome) is disheartening even to the most determined. If there were an alternative route to fulfilling my educational need, I would approach it without delay.
>
> Courtesy and helpfulness in the admissions office would ease the pressure of getting through the mountain of red tape.
>
> The university I attend needs to develop a better system for registering and changing classes. It does not begin to compare with the one at the community college. The counselors and teachers need to be much friendlier to all students.
>
> Efforts should be made to aid older transfer and returning students in entering honors programs.

> I was made to feel unwelcome when applying to enter the honors program despite having made *A*'s in two semesters of honors English at the community college and transferring with a GPA of 3.91.

Other comments emphasized the need for universities to do a better job of dealing with the needs of older students. Their advice assumes special importance when considered in the light of the tendency for minority students to be older and to have more family responsibilities than nonminority students, as reported earlier in this chapter:

> I think most university officials will agree that a great number of working adults are returning to school. Yet, most universities still gear the majority of their undergraduate degree programs to the full-time student. I would like to see more undergraduate degree programs offered in the evening college or a more widespread use of the weekend college concept.
>
> I would suggest that universities offer more academic courses during the night so students can work during the day and study at night without any academic problems or conflicts.
>
> The parking garages are isolated, especially at night. There has been much talk of muggings and rape in these areas. Although security guards are available, I am concerned about the walk from my car to class. Also, the secluded areas of the library present a threat. This university is located in the inner city, which is more easily accessible to "disturbed" people.

System-Level Concerns. A number of comments dealt with policies usually implemented at the coordinating board level. One common theme dealt with differences in academic calendars for community colleges and universities, credits for common courses, and course labeling; these were all variables that complicated transfer and caused loss of credit or unnecessary repetition of content:

> One area where improvement is needed is the transitional process changing between semesters and quarters. Unfortunately, I cannot suggest any way to improve this situation.
>
> At the community college, each course is worth three points whereas at the university, they are four points. At the university you need eight credits per field of study. Therefore, when transferring, even though the community college credits are accepted, you still may have to take an extra course to fulfill distribution requirements.
>
> The classes I took in my major at the community college wouldn't all transfer because at the community college the classes were in home economics and at the university they're in education. So now I'm retaking classes (that have proven to be the same) at the university that I already took at the community college, causing me to have to go an extra year to get my bachelor's degree.
>
> Let students know what credits are acceptable and what credits aren't. Many students take courses they don't need to transfer and end up with "credits in the air," as we call it. Nothing makes a student more upset than finding out that the credits they worked to earn at the community college aren't accepted at the university to which they wish to transfer.

Other student comments focused on problems involving financial aid and the effect of entrance examinations on the older returning student:

> An effort should be made to aid older transfer and returning students in attaining financial aid. Most scholarships were geared to graduating high school students.
>
> I feel that a student who graduated from a junior college over fourteen years ago should not be made to take the entrance examination. I have not yet heard from the university on whether I have been admitted, and I have already earned eighteen credit hours there.

Conclusion

There is a tendency to view the survivors of the transfer process who responded to our survey as examples of the success of the system. The comments of two "successful" transfers provide insight into the battle that remains for many:

> The freedom I had at the community college is nonexistent at the university. I feel lost and I feel like a loser; don't care how hard I try. I only get a *C;* this is frustrating to me. I'm on academic warning. This spring quarter is my last try. If I don't pass or do well, I'm going to wait until my kids can support themselves; then I will go back.
>
> I do not know if this applies to other people; I had a terrible time trying to get used to my new school. It was very difficult to get even a *B* grade during my first term. I thought I would not make it, but after I spoke to some people about my problems, I found out that I was not different and by my second term I improved. I got all *B*'s and an *A* grade.

In concluding this chapter, it is only fair to note that 35 percent of those returning surveys chose not to respond to the optional open-response item. An additional 8 percent provided positive comments about the transfer experience. So overall the transfer process works and probably works well for close to half of those who experience it. But that still leaves more than half who think that the process could be improved. While such improvements would benefit all students, the least experienced and least well prepared would benefit the most. Minority students appear disproportionately concentrated in the half that could benefit from the improvements suggested.

The comparison of data yielded by the survey, along with the information provided through interviews and document analysis, suggests close agreement about the issues among all participants. The comments of students generally conform to those of knowledgeable actors within the institutions and on the state coordinating boards. But given a reasonable level of consensus about the way the system works and the impact that it has on students, what can be done to improve degree opportunities for urban students in general and minority students in particular? Many of those interviewed identified programs that they believed were working well. They also spoke of interventions that they wanted to try. Their insights and suggestions are reported in Chapter Eight.

8

Improving Transfer Programs and Practices

In the preceding chapters, we have characterized community colleges and universities as conflicting cultures because their dominant values differ, as do the practices that grow out of those values. We have also suggested that the differences in culture have an adverse impact on the baccalaureate achievement of urban minority students who begin their postsecondary education in community colleges.

For urban students the light at the end of the transfer tunnel may appear at times to be an onrushing train. The uncertain nature of their experience is not always easy for outsiders to understand, particularly if such outsiders view it from the perspective of articulation agreements and state policies designed to make more or less autonomous institutions behave as if they were part of a system. Universities and community colleges operate within state contexts that presume cooperation. Legislatures and state coordinating boards have implicit or explicit policies promoting the free exchange of students among public institutions with minimum loss of credit. Political leaders in urban settings subscribe to the American dream of upward mobility without regard to race or socioeconomic circumstances. And there is the expectation that public institutions will contribute not only to the realization of that dream but also to improving the quality of life within the cities in which they are located.

The term most often used to describe the activities through which community colleges and universities cooperate to encourage student progress toward the baccalaureate degree is *articulation.* In this chapter, we begin by describing state policies promoting cooperation and the institutional responses to these policies in the form of program designs and supporting services. We then consider the perceptions of college and university staff members of the barriers that remain and the most promising strategies for overcoming those barriers.

State Policies on Articulation

While legislatures sometimes react to problems involving loss of credit or deficiencies in student performance by passing laws that set minimum standards, the major sources of state-level articulation policies are coordinating boards, particularly those with regulatory powers. Coordinating boards place pressure on baccalaureate institutions to honor the academic transfer work of community colleges and upon community colleges to maintain academic standards comparable to those found in four-year institutions.

Unfortunately, state-legislated or -regulated policies do not guarantee effective transfer. Articulation in its most essential form calls for cooperation, and too often participating institutions will cooperate only when it suits their own interests. So actual cooperation, as distinct from the legislated variety, is governed first by the law of supply and demand, and, second, by the personality and preferences of those involved in the process. For example, when there are too few high school graduates to maintain desired enrollment levels, articulation improves; when personalities clash, articulation deteriorates.

The tone for the implementation of articulation policies is established by institutional leaders. When strong leaders emphasize the importance of institutional cooperation, policies work. But when institutional leaders are lukewarm or even hostile toward institutional cooperation, policies have little bearing on the transfer opportunities actually provided to individual students.

The policies among states participating in the study can be described in terms of the typology of articulation policies developed by Kintzer and Wattenbarger (1985). Florida, Illinois, and Texas represent examples of states where formal and legally based policies govern the articulation process. In Florida, such policies define general education requirements for two- and four-year institutions, specify the times when required courses can be offered at each level, and designate services to aid the movement of students through the system. There is also a statewide common calendar and a uniform course-numbering system, as well as a prohibition against requiring students to take lower-division general education courses if they have previously completed a prescribed general education program in another institution. Florida also requires all lower-division students to complete a College-Level Academic Skills Test before granting them permission to continue in upper-division studies at a public university.

Illinois requires two-year colleges to establish admission criteria for their baccalaureate programs comparable to those established by four-year colleges and universities. There is also a compact requiring associate degree graduates from state community colleges to be accepted in public universities with upper-division standing. Texas has established a basic core of general academic courses that can be transferred freely among all public institutions.

Arizona, Missouri, and New Jersey are states that concentrate on formulas for equating credits in general education and in the major while exhibiting less concern about supporting services. New Jersey, for example, provides a "full-faith-and-credit" plan that guarantees graduates of approved transfer programs that their general education credits will be accepted in their entirety toward the general education requirements of a New Jersey public university (not necessarily the one of choice).

Missouri provides guidelines that set forth "the expected course of action or set of circumstances that apply to decision making in which transfer of credits is involved" (Missouri Coordinating Board for Higher Education, 1984, p. 2). Graduates of two-year associate in arts or associate in science degrees are guaranteed junior standing provided that they have pursued a program mutually agreed upon by the community college and the university and have earned the appropriate degree.

Arizona has an articulation committee jointly appointed by the Arizona Board of Regents and the State Community College Board. This committee operates through program subcommittees comprised of discipline-based faculty members who have the responsibility for identifying and resolving the entire range of problems that have an impact on effective transfer. A Course Equivalency Guide is also published annually, and some institutions exchange curriculum representatives.

The Kintzer and Wattenbarger typology breaks down, however, when it is applied to Pennsylvania and Ohio. Pennsylvania straddles two categories; that is, it has a mixture of state system policies and individual agreements among institutions that creates an articulation environment too complex to describe here. Ohio, like Pennsylvania, has a combination of state system policies and agreements among individual institutions. While Ohio, like Missouri, has a statement on guidelines for articulation that was adopted by the Board of Regents, the statement stops short of defining the expected course of action by institutions, suggesting instead a program of voluntary compliance among them.

Despite variations in the regulatory environment, all states had some form of articulation agreement to govern transfer between two- and four-year institutions. Sometimes the agreements were the product of negotiations between individual institutions; in other cases, they were prescribed, at least in a general way, by coordinating board directives. But even in states with formal and legally based policies, the reality of institutional relationships was often at variance with the intent of policy. In one state, for example, a major receiving university had never accepted a state compact and continued the practice of defining its articulation policy on a college-by-college basis. Because of the wide variation in the preparation of students being admitted from the community colleges with which the university regularly interacted, this resistance to the statewide policy was implicitly accepted by coordinating board officials.

As noted earlier, the reality of articulation practices is determined not by the semantic content of written policies or agreements but by the concern and commitment exhibited by institutional leaders. In this section, we have provided some general sense of state influences on interinstitutional relationships. We turn now to a consideration of programmatic attempts to deal with articulation issues and to a discussion of some of the services provided by states and institutions to aid student movement from community college to university.

Transfer Programs

Community colleges typically offer four different associate degree programs. The most widely offered, the associate in arts degree, involves completion of sixty to sixty-four semester hours of credit and conforms, in general, to the lower-division requirements of the baccalaureate degree in most fields where specialization does not begin until the junior year. The associate in science degree, also widely offered, follows the pattern of the associate in arts degree but places greater emphasis on math and science to prepare transfer students for majors in these areas or in engineering. Virtually all community colleges offer these two degrees.

The associate in applied science degree generally requires completion of more credit hours than the two transfer-oriented degrees; approximately two-thirds of the required work must be in an area of specialization and the remaining one-third must be devoted to general education. This degree is intended to prepare students for immediate employment in a career field after leaving the community college or to upgrade students in a field where they are already employed. All the community colleges we visited offered this degree or some close variation of it.

Most urban colleges also offer an associate in general

studies degree. This degree requires completion of sixty to sixty-four semester hours but has few or no distribution requirements and often permits the inclusion of a specified number of remedial credits. Except for permitting the award of a credential to students completing an almost random selection of courses, the purpose of the degree is unclear, and no community college recommends the degree for students interested in transfer. Nevertheless, students have appeared at university admissions offices with this degree and objected when they did not receive the junior standing awarded for the more restrictive associate in arts or associate in science programs.

A variety of program designs were observed among the transfer curricula. In states with more formalized articulation agreements, the tendency was to specify a core or general education component for the lower division. This was sometimes described as a two-plus-two design, with upper-division institutions agreeing to accept core general education courses as satisfying their lower-division requirements for a baccalaureate degree. Community college administrators highly approved of the core concept for developing institution-to-institution articulation agreements because it provided substantial flexibility in curriculum design.

In cases where state coordinating agencies had less regulatory authority or assumed a more consultative role, articulation agreements often were negotiated on a major-by-major basis. This model required consultation among faculty members from universities and community colleges to determine the type, level, and sequence of lower-division courses transferable for each major, including those courses to be treated as electives and those meeting specialization requirements.

The full-faith-and-credit policy described earlier assumed a comparability of lower-division courses regardless of where they were offered. Course comparability in this setting was determined by a panel of faculty members from affected institutions. In other states, the determination was made through an analysis of catalogue descriptions or course outlines and was closely controlled by university faculty members. Regardless of articulation agreements, the question of which credits applied toward a degree and which counted as electives was determined in the university at the department level. This approach, of course, gave final authority to faculty in the university to determine course content, standards of performance, and credit worth.

Community college administrators have not been happy with the degree of influence over their curricula exercised by university faculty through the process of evaluating courses for transfer. Their effort to gain increased autonomy has taken several forms, including (1) a push to gain acceptance for specialized courses offered in the associate in applied science degrees and (2) ambiguous labeling of courses, which places the burden of determining course transferability on the university. In general, students have experienced the fewest problems when following the most closely prescribed programs. While greater curricular autonomy has undoubtedly served the needs of many community college clients, it has contributed to the problems experienced by those seeking baccalaureate degrees.

In contrast to general studies programs, capstone programs (also called two-plus-two programs in some settings) have enhanced opportunities for transfer by making it possible for students to build an upper-division sequence on specialized work completed in the community college. This allows a student with an applied associate degree to earn the baccalaureate degree in an additional two years. In recent years, capstone programs have been developed in such areas as allied health and the technologies. Capstone programs are quite rare in research universities but relatively common in comprehensive universities. They are always available in the upper-division comprehensive universities because such institutions rely on community college preparation in the lower division for any major they offer.

Where research universities offered capstone programs, it was often in response to the pressures of a state coordinating board that had required the program as a condition for approving a new degree. Interestingly, four universities offered capstone programs in nursing, a field that is generally regarded as unpromising for this approach because of perceived opposition from the National League for Nursing. Other capstone programs were found in law enforcement, hotel/motel and restaurant management, computer science, and art. However, capstone programs appeared to lead a tenuous existence, as university faculty prefer to admit their own freshmen. Their resistance to programs making them dependent on community college faculty for lower-division preparation was not dissimilar to the resistance of community college administrators to the influence on their transfer programs exercised by university faculty.

University faculty may accept capstone programs to secure approval for a new bachelor's degree program; once such approval has been granted, however, their efforts turn to securing approval for admitting high school graduates directly to the program. If these efforts are crowned with success, barriers to smooth progression to junior status soon appear for the community college transfers. Among research universities where capstone programs had been initiated under duress, the programs either were not working well or were in a state of transition. The major exception to this generalization involved bachelor of technology programs built on the applied science degree in engineering-related fields.

One comprehensive university did offer a second option, namely, the open university degree. While there are many variations on this program, all permit students substantial flexibility in counting credit from previous work. Some may also award credit for life experience. With the assistance of an adviser, students develop a contract with the university that specifies an appropriate objective and an acceptable plan for achieving that objective. Some programs require completion of a minimum number of hours in residence, but this requirement can usually be fulfilled through extension courses, courses offered on television, or other arrangements designed to avoid disruption in the student's job or family life. As one example, students who graduated in auto mechanics from a community college were able to earn the baccalaureate degree with full credit applied from their auto mechanics program. Several faculty members teaching in the auto mechanics program at the community college had earned this same degree.

In spite of important value differences between community colleges and universities, they have both given attention to program practices that would improve opportunities for student movement. In addition to efforts aimed at the design of compatible programs, a variety of advising tools and services were available in many settings. For example, most universities published curriculum guides through which they guaranteed the acceptance of specified courses offered by a community college as long as a *C* grade was earned. In at least two states, universities and community colleges operated according to a common calendar. In one metropolitan area, a common transcript had been developed by a consortium of two- and four-year institutions to facilitate admissions and placement decisions and to maintain continuity in the award of financial aid. A community college district and a university in another city were preparing to implement the electronic transfer of credits and had approved a consortium agreement that kept students concurrently enrolled in both institutions eligible for financial assistance even though such students would not have been eligible based on the total number of credits taken at either institution independently.

One state-level articulation agreement provided a mechanism to resolve student or institutional grievances arising from the transfer of credits. Representatives from colleges and universities met regularly with their counterparts from the state office to review articulation practices and to deal with problems. A common practice was to appoint an individual with specific responsibilities for maintaining good relationships with an adjacent community college or university and for resolving articulation problems as these were identified.

Up to this point, we have identified state and institutional policies and practices designed to keep the system open for those it was intended to serve. In the next two sections of this chapter, we report barriers to transfer as these were perceived by staff members in community colleges and universities.

Barriers: The Community College Perspective

The barriers identified by community college faculty and administrators centered on the attitudes and practices of university staff members, as well as on the preparation of students coming to the community college. The relative absence of self-criticism could have been a normal reaction to outsiders who were questioning institutional practice, or it could have resulted from an absence of evaluative data. But whatever the reason, few community college-based respondents saw articulation barriers as a consequence of community college attitudes or practices.

Criticism of University Attitudes and Practices. University administrators and faculty members were consistently criticized for their condescending attitudes toward community colleges. The president of an urban community college who had assumed her position a year earlier reported no welcoming communication or any subsequent contact from the president of a nearby public university. She observed, "I guess it is my responsibility to initiate contact; apparently he [the university president] is too busy to extend a welcome or to discuss ways in which we might work together. I have seen him in several group meetings, but I am sure he didn't even recognize me." The dean of a college of arts and sciences agreed that the attitudes of faculty members represented a major problem: "University faculty view community colleges and their products as inferior. While the data contradict that view, the attitude persists. Interestingly, community colleges defend themselves on the basis of data, but it doesn't change the attitude of university faculty at all."

University faculty members were described as unfairly critical of those who teach in community colleges. Some community college faculty members said their university counterparts did not understand the community college mission and were themselves so preoccupied by the need to "publish or perish" that their views of the teaching function were reactionary. One faculty member added, "It's ludicrous that they [the English faculty] have been criticizing us for the level of preparation of our students. First of all, three of us are employed there as adjunct faculty members, and two-thirds of us completed our graduate training with them!"

Community college English faculty were especially critical of the research university practice of staffing composition courses almost exclusively with teaching assistants. In cases where universities accepted *D* grades awarded by their own teaching assistants while refusing to accept *D*'s from the community college, the criticism turned into hostility. To offset adverse reactions from community college faculty, several universities no longer accept *D* grades for courses in the major regardless of where the grade was earned.

Community college staff members also criticized university policies that encouraged students to transfer early despite the considerable body of evidence that relates persistence and achievement to the number of hours completed at a community college before transferring. Another source of concern involved changes in university programs or admission practices that were made without sufficient advance notice to affected community colleges. One university instituted a writing test for transfer students and required those who did poorly on it to enroll in a special writing course. Community college leaders demanded that the requirement be removed or that native as well as transfer students be tested. Eventually the university agreed to test its own students as well as transfers.

In a different university, faculty decided to change the mathematics sequence without conferring with community college staff who were using the university's curriculum guides to advise students. The director of admissions unwittingly poured fuel on the controversy by declaring that the catalogue governing university requirements was the last one printed prior to a student's matriculation. He added, "There is no consideration for students who follow the catalogue in effect at the time they begin in a community college." In this situation, community college faculty members and administrators were ready to encourage their students to challenge the university through the courts.

Community college student affairs personnel were frequently critical of university policies for their absence of concern about the background and needs of transfer students. They argued that universities should establish practices designed to facilitate transition from the more supportive community college environment to the university environment. One counselor observed, "They think their bulletin boards and the printed materials lying around are tantamount to effective counseling and advisement. They simply don't understand that our students lack the middle-class orientation and are not self-directed or self-confident."

Student Preparation. Even though the question about barriers produced substantial criticism of university policies and practices, for most respondents the single most important impediment to effective transfer was student preparation. And in discussions of this concern, there was at least implicit criticism of community college practices. One humanities division chair noted, "The principal barrier to transfer for our students is that the reading, writing, and mathematics skills not learned in high school are not learned at the community college either." He continued, "Teachers have learned to teach content without requiring students to read or write."

While problems with basic skills were pervasive, community college faculty members were also concerned about student attitudes and motivation. Staff members pointed to the difficulty of communicating to minority students, in the absence of role models, the difference that higher education could make in their lives. There was a general sense that encouraging students below the poverty level to defer immediate gratification in the hope of future rewards represented an almost hopeless challenge.

Barriers: The University Perspective

While the central barrier perceived by those in community colleges involved the attitudes of university personnel, the central barrier perceived by universities involved the quality of students. When reduced to its lowest possible denominator, "quality" meant well-prepared, independent learners who reflected the middle-class values of scholarship and inquiry.

At the extreme, the suggested way to ensure such quality was to eliminate the community college experience entirely. A vice-president of academic affairs at one urban university declared:

> The policy that inhibits successful baccalaureate programs is the state requirement for the majority

> of academic high school graduates to go through the community college system. It is quite evident that the policy is inappropriate when you consider the fact a higher percentage of high school graduates from this region of the state actually go to institutions out of state. This is because they want to avoid going to the community colleges.

The same administrator indicated that community colleges were an appropriate point of access for minorities, although he was not sure whether enough minorities were achieving such access.

Quality concerns of universities also focused on grading practices. Several university administrators suggested that community colleges used grades as an incentive device for improving the self-concept of minority students rather than as standards against which to measure student achievement. As noted elsewhere, community college faculty members conceded that they did use norm-referenced grading systems in contrast to the more criterion-referenced systems commonly used in universities.

University faculty and administrators also pointed to differences in course content as a barrier to successful transfer. Those in arts and sciences criticized the lack of depth in community college courses. Several observed that community college faculty did not cover the same content even when they used the same text. University faculty in specialized areas were sometimes critical of the perspective from which community college courses were taught. One business faculty member commented, "They teach that course from a sociological perspective, but we teach it from an economic perspective. Their students are simply out of sync with ours."

A somewhat different perspective was offered by an associate dean of engineering: "Community college faculty have no adequate understanding of where their courses lead at the upper division. They need some sense of what higher-level courses are all about if they really want continuity for their students." This comment closely paraphrased a student comment reported in the previous chapter. Again, a vice-president of academic affairs explained why he taught a freshman-level chemistry class on alternate years and an advanced course during the intervening years. The freshman course reacquainted him with lower-division clientele and the subject matter:

> [This led me] to rethink my own approach and to examine a strategy to make these students actually think through what they are studying. Community college faculty who never have an opportunity to teach the subsequent course in a sequence are vulnerable to teaching without examining whether they are maintaining the rigor and standards which are needed.

While university personnel did identify course content, grading standards, and continuity as potential barriers to effective transfer, their general attitude toward articulation was one of complacency. In contrast to that of university personnel, the predominant reaction among community college faculty and administrators was one of frustration. This difference is a consequence of the control that universities exercise over the articulation process. As one result, they are able to protect themselves against community college practices they dislike without jeopardizing the flow of needed students. The use of such simple expedients as selectively granting elective credit or administering validation exams presents an inconvenience to transfers from suburban community colleges. Urban community colleges, by contrast, experienced these practices as serious impediments to the progress of their clientele and were critical of the attitudes that led to additional difficulties for an already high-risk population.

Community College Articulation Proposals

Community college administrators and faculty recommended a combination of internal reforms and changes in university practices to improve student opportunities for trouble-free transfer. One proposed reform illustrated the differing impacts of current practice on inner-city and suburban institutions. In one district, the white president of a suburban community college observed, "People don't pay much attention to the transfer program: it's working." The black administrator of a sister inner-city college emphasized the need for a two-tier transfer program with selective admissions for the upper tier while maintaining open admissions to the lower. Other proposals for internal reforms paralleled many of the strategies for improving student achievement discussed in Chapter Three. Included were honors programs, stronger liberal arts programs, more competency-based outcomes, and released time for faculty members to coordinate liberal arts offerings.

Administrators emphasized a number of practices: providing students with realistic information about themselves and their alternatives at the time of admission, helping students identify objectives early and assisting them to develop individual educational plans, working to help students raise expectations of themselves, and ensuring that information about transfer opportunities and requirements reached students prior to their first registration. Administrators also emphasized the need for community college faculty and counselors to visit four-year institutions.

Administrators also pointed to the need to improve faculty advising, to require high standards of students, and to enhance learning support systems and financial aid. They added that students should not be required to choose between meeting the graduation requirements of a community college catalogue or following the transfer guide published by a four-year institution. And despite protests to the contrary from some top administrators, there was a clear sense among faculty and middle-level managers that community colleges in general, and inner-city colleges in particular, placed excessive emphasis on vocational education to the detriment of the transfer function.

Beyond actions that community colleges might take to strengthen the transfer function, a number of needed changes in university practices were also identified. Perhaps the most fundamental was the need for improved communication with community colleges. Suggested forms of communication included clear-cut statements on transfer policy, visits by program representatives to improve advising for potential majors, closer working relationships between university counselors and their community college counterparts, faculty exchanges, and direct and continuing feedback on the performance of transfer students. None of these proposals were revolutionary, and all were found in operation in one or more of the participating cities. Most of these practices represented exceptions, however, and none of the pairs of institutions were involved in a systematic effort to implement the entire range of practices identified as beneficial. For example, a majority of the universities relied upon the Family Privacy Act (Buckley amendment) as a rationale for providing summary statistics or none at all on the performance of community college transfers. Illustrating the importance of individual action in making articulation work, one university vice-president received a request from a community college district for student-specific data. His request to university legal counsel produced an opinion acknowledging that there were exceptions in the act dealing with research and the improvement of educational programs but concluding with the admonition, "If you want to be absolutely safe, we suggest you withhold the information." Deciding against being "absolutely safe," the vice-president directed that the information be provided, and he thereby established a continuing dialogue that led to the exchange of data tapes each semester in a form suitable for follow-up studies. Eventually, in fact, the two staffs decided to implement the electronic exchange of transcripts.

It must be noted that it was not always the university that blocked the feedback on transfer student performance. In one city, a university institutional research office offered to provide this data. But the community college district, which was operating in a sensitive political environment, indicated informally that it was not interested. The unstated reason was that such information would reflect adversely on the declining performance of students attending an inner-city college, a situation that the district preferred not to publicize or confront. With the exception of one state where the legislature had mandated that public universities provide regular feedback information and the university described above, only two other universities voluntarily provided information. Unfortunately, that information was less systematic and less comprehensive than community colleges needed if they were to improve their transfer programs.

Faculty exchanges were widely identified as the single most promising strategy for reducing transfer barriers. Where contacts did exist between university and community college faculty, those involved were uniformly positive and reported that such contacts not only enhanced university faculty views of community college programs but also provided leadership in strengthening community college articulation practices. However, motivating faculty members from research universities to devote additional time to teaching-related activities when they believe that they are already burdened with more teaching responsibilities than their research interests can accommodate constitutes a major challenge. The two universities that had made the greatest strides in coping with this issue were both recipients of external grants that provided incentives for joint activity among university and community college faculty and, in one instance, high school faculty as well. The area of faculty exchange would appear to be a particularly promising one for intervention by foundations interested in promoting more effective articulation between universities and community colleges.

Outside of joint teaching activities, several promising forms of cooperation were identified. In one setting, where community college faculty became suspicious of the way in which the university graded writing samples that were used to place native and transfer students in a composition sequence, it was agreed that samples would be evaluated by both groups with joint resolution where serious differences occurred. In other settings, universities invited faculty members from a community college to sit on committees dealing with the revision of admission requirements and the construction of an exam for advanced placement. In one setting, they were asked to serve on college-level curriculum committees. These experiences suggest that the two most reliable ways for quieting criticism of university practices are participation and equity. Universities that involved community college faculty in design or evaluation and treated community college transfers the same way they treated their own native students received high marks for their efforts to improve articulation.

Finally, from a community college perspective there were actions that should be taken by state coordinating boards to improve opportunities for minority students to earn the baccalaureate degree. One such action involved redefining institutional missions to limit competition among public institutions. In those states where this had not been done, community college and university personnel saw competition for students as one of the most serious barriers to effective transfer. Also important from the community college perspective was giving preferred status to the transfer associate degree by guaranteeing those who earned it junior status without the course-by-course evaluation typically applied to those transferring without a degree. In states where the associate degree was given preferred status, more students graduated from community colleges, and articulation procedures appeared to function more smoothly. In general, community college administrators favored a stronger coordinating board role in mandating articulation practices.

University Articulation Proposals

As previously noted, universities controlled the articulation process and so were better satisfied with existing arrangements than were their community college colleagues. Without exception, universities resented intrusions from state coordinating boards, however well meaning, and were particularly opposed to having them exert greater influence over the curriculum. Reflecting their satisfaction with current procedures, universities advanced relatively few suggestions for improvement.

Chief among the suggestions that they did advance, however, was the need for faculty and counselors in community colleges to better prepare minority students for the university's culture and expectations. One university dean observed, "Most community college transfer students come to us expecting things to be done for them; we expect them to be self-directed and independent." But sometimes student behavior can be misinterpreted. Speaking of transfer students from a predominantly minority community college, a dean in a different urban university noted, "The students from community college arrive here feeling they know all about university campus life. They are so independent they never seem to ask questions or to come to us seeking help." Review of the statistics for this university revealed an extremely high attrition rate for minority transfer students the first semester after admission. Clearly, there were explanations other than a spirit of independence for the lack of minority student use of university services.

Faculty members expressed concern that students frequently came to the university without completing math requirements, thus eliminating themselves from many of the more desirable majors and inviting problems with course sequencing. In reflecting their concern with standards, several administrators and faculty members suggested that community colleges implement assessment procedures and withhold grades until specified levels of performance had been achieved. One department chairman observed, "If they would only recognize the importance of quality control at their end of the line, we'd be happy to accept their students." A faculty member at another university declared, "They really need to institute a writing requirement across the curriculum because that's the only way their students will ever learn to write."

At two universities, staff members proposed that community colleges institute an ongoing process of program review and institutional self-study for their transfer programs similar to the process used by specialized and institutional accrediting agencies. The self-study process would involve not only community college faculty and administrators but representatives from universities as well. One university administrator suggested that the state coordinating board should require such self-study in the absence of action by local institutions to initiate such a process.

While university staff were not reluctant to provide advice to their community college counterparts, much of what they said applied to their own internal practices as well. Several universities did not have adequate curriculum guides for transfer students even though university staff directly involved in the articulation process felt that such guides were essential and that their preparation and maintenance should be an assigned responsibility. Staff members were also critical of the absence of systematic procedures for determining course equivalencies and for reviewing transcript credits.

Some university administrators suggested that universities should accept or reject transfer students outright rather than subject them to rules and regulations designed to impede and discourage them. Mentioned as particularly problematic were the recalculation of grade point averages on the basis of different rules from those applied in the community college and the excessive award of elective credits in the departmental evaluation of transcripts.

Underlying most of the suggestions for improving articulation was an evident need for greater communication between community colleges and universities. One dean noted, "If we could just develop a sense of collegiality between university and community college faculty, 90 percent of the problems would go away." Complicating the challenge of developing such a sense of collegiality was the difference between those who identified problems and those who were in a position to do something about them. Administrators of university programs for minority students often held views of articulation not significantly different from those in community colleges, but senior administrators and faculty members were much less aware of these issues and less inclined to see them as problems requiring priority attention.

Conclusion

One of the assumptions that governed the design of this study was that those who established public urban community colleges and urban universities in the same cities at about the same point in time had some expectation that the two institutions would work together. And, in fact, we found reasonable levels of cooperation in more than half of the cities studied. In all states, formal articulation policies, some emanating from the state and others from the local institution, were designed to accomplish an orderly progression from lower-division to upper-division work.

Regardless of the state role, however, the articulation process was controlled at the operational level by senior institutions, a reality resented by community colleges. It was not uncommon for university administrators to take the position stated by one dean, "Bureaucratic attempts at articulation are largely doomed to failure." This position was, of course, consistent with the preference of universities to limit the influence of the state coordinating boards on their curriculum. It was also consistent with the limited influence that administrators typically exerted over the curriculum within the university setting.

The variation in articulation practices found among institutions participating in the study could not be satisfactorily explained by the differences in the policies established by state coordinating boards. One research university, because of its history and institutional mission, had developed a positive relationship with the community college in its city despite the absence of formal policies, meetings, or agreements at the state level. This type of "best practice relationship," however, was heavily dependent on the personalities of responsible administrators.

A second university developed a positive relationship with an adjacent urban community college by setting policies and assigning resources to the task. This university was aided in its efforts by state-level policies and machinery that both encouraged attention to the problems of transfer students and provided a way of dealing with the inevitable snags. But state policies and institutional agreements, while helpful, are not sufficient to achieve effective transfer in the absence of commitment from key university staff. Where there was an absence of such commitment or where relationships between top university and community college administrators were strained or hostile, institutions subverted the most detailed and carefully defined state articulation policies and ignored any institutional agreements that were in existence.

There are some things that community colleges can do to help their students. For example, they can define transfer programs more clearly and place emphasis on exit competencies. There are also actions that universities can take: they can improve communication with community colleges, they can eliminate unnecessary scrutiny of transcripts at the department level, and they can place more emphasis on articulation as a priority. Because articulation works reasonably well from a university perspective and from the perspective of suburban community college administrators, there is the danger of accepting current practice as satisfactory. Unfortunately, there appears to be much in current practice that impacts adversely on inner-city colleges and the heavily minority student populations who attend them.

9

Assessing the Urban Educational Pipeline

We began by posing a series of policy questions concerning the actions of state coordinating boards, public universities, and community colleges in assisting or impeding progress to the baccalaureate degree for students who began their postsecondary experience in an urban community college. We focused on urban community colleges and universities because they serve a high proportion of all minority students enrolled in most state systems. Of course, urban institutions serve students from a variety of racial and ethnic backgrounds, as evidenced by the fact that minority students were the predominant clientele in only three of the universities and only nine of the community college campuses that we visited.

This chapter summarizes our answers to the questions that drove this study. These answers represent informed judgments about an extremely complex set of policy issues rather than empirically based findings. Because the questions were intentionally broad and the data from institutions and states unintentionally fragmented and incomplete, we have included in the discussion, wherever possible, studies reported by states in addition to those we visited.

Student Objectives and Academic Preparation

The proportion of students currently enrolled in an urban community college who are potential candidates for transfer to a four-year institution depends on the demographics of the college as well as on the policies of the state in which the college is located. States such as Florida and California, which restrict student choice through limiting the number of freshmen that public universities are authorized to admit, cause more first-time, full-time freshmen—the prime transfer population—to enroll in community colleges. In contrast, community colleges that enroll high proportions of part-time and underprepared students have fewer transfers simply because students in these categories are less likely to transfer.

A national study (Center for the Study of Community Colleges, 1985) of twenty-four comprehensive community colleges in which minority and low-income students represented at least one-third of the total enrollments reported a difference of 11 percentage points between Asians, who had the highest transfer attitudes (61 percent), and blacks, who had the lowest (50 percent). In between were whites (60 percent) and Hispanics (58 percent). The comparable figures for high-transfer behaviors were Asians (24 percent), whites (20 percent), Hispanics (15 percent), and blacks (12 percent). These figures, as previously noted, are remarkably similar to the estimates furnished by faculty and administrators in our study institutions, who indicated that 40 to 50 percent of their entering students had transfer as a primary objective and that 7 to 20 percent of those with this objective might also have the necessary academic preparation and persistence to achieve it.

A City University of New York (CUNY) study of long-term graduation rates from community colleges for open admission students (Lavin, Murtha, and Kaufman, 1984) found that 24 percent of black and Hispanic students graduated over the eleven years that they were followed. The comparable rates for regular students (those with high school averages of 75 or better) from these same two minority groups were 39 and 37 percent. Judging by the percentage of students needing remediation, those attending inner-city colleges in this study more closely resembled the open admission students of CUNY than they did the regular admittees.

One of the units of CUNY, an inner-city community college with a high proportion of minority students, many of whom required remedial assistance, followed first-time freshmen over seven academic semesters. In the study, success was defined as graduation or the completion of twenty semester hours with a grade point average of 2.0. The institution tested all entering students and required those deficient in reading, writing, or math to undergo remediation. More than 95 percent of those who entered required remediation in one or more of the basic skills areas. Those who completed remediation successfully did not perform in ways significantly different from those who did not require remediation (Borough of Manhattan Community College, 1983).

The success rate for first-time entering freshmen in need of remediation in the study was about 20 percent. Combining those who did not need remediation with those who completed the remediation sequence successfully yields a maximum potential transfer population of less than 30 percent. Since the modal student in many community colleges has been described as "an adult taking only a single course and not interested in earning a degree," the 30 percent maximum estimate must be applied to the less than half of the student population with baccalaureate aspirations who enroll for at least six semester hours each term.

One of the best systems for assessing student preparation in the nation has been developed by New Jersey. The state also publishes each year a study of the outcomes of assessment and remediation. The most recent report (New Jersey Basic Skills Council, 1986) documents student preparation and its impact on subsequent academic success. Overall, 48 percent of the students entering community colleges in the fall of 1983 required remediation in one or more of the four areas assessed by the New Jersey Basic Skills Test (reading, writing, computation, and elementary algebra). On the average, 41 percent of those who needed remediation in one or more of the four areas did not complete it within four semesters. For this group the successful survival rate, calculated by determining how many of the entering cohort remained enrolled with a grade point average of *C* or better in the spring of 1985, was a dismal 13 percent.

Among those entering Essex County College during the same period, more than 83 percent required remediation and 74 percent of those who needed it failed to complete it. Successful survival rates even for those who did not need remediation, were well below state averages, reflecting some of the special problems faced by inner-city colleges.

Students do transfer without completing four semesters at a community college. But studies show consistently that half to two-thirds of all transfers from all community colleges hold an associate degree. In California, for example, both the master plan for higher education and the policies of the University of California system emphasize junior status as the preferred transfer credential. In the State University of New York (SUNY) system, a board policy mandates special consideration for associate in arts and associate in science graduates. Most transfers hold one of these credentials, although many also transfer with occupational degrees. But the difference in transfer rates is striking. While the SUNY community colleges award almost twice as many degrees in occupational fields as they do in the transfer categories, students are more than twice as likely to transfer from the associate in arts and associate in science degree programs than from those in occupational fields. And 60 percent of all transfer students in SUNY have the associate degree when they transfer (Lavin, 1986).

In our survey 76 percent of the Hispanics and 61 percent of the blacks held the associate degree at the time they transferred. The comparable figures for whites and Asians were 48 and 32 percent. Putting all this information together, our estimate of the potential transfer students in urban colleges would not exceed under the best of conditions 20 percent of all those enrolled for six or more credit hours. Indeed, this figure is the estimate for the state of California provided by the state chancellor's office (California Community Colleges, 1984), using the same base that we suggest (six or more credit hours and intending to transfer). Depending on the demographics of a specific institution, the figures might be as low as 5 percent. Of course, these estimates represent potential rather than actual figures.

From these studies and other available information, it would appear that about half of those entering urban community colleges entertain aspirations for the baccalaureate degree even though fewer than half of those with such aspirations engage in the behaviors associated with successful transfer. There is more variation in preparation and behaviors among the different racial groups than there is in aspirations. Colleges that enroll high proportions of blacks and Hispanics have the least favorable ratios of potential transfers, with the proportion of those with adequate preparation ranging as low as 5 percent of those enrolled for six credit hours or more. Even in those institutions with the least favorable ratios of prospective transfers, however, one-fifth of the students needing remediation complete a prescribed sequence successfully. And after completing such a sequence, they perform in ways similar to those who entered with adequate preparation.

Transfer Behavior

Among those with appropriate academic behaviors who have transfer as an objective, three major variables influence who actually transfers and when. The first involves distance and travel barriers. The greater the difficulty in reaching a university, the more credits a student will earn before transferring. In contrast, in urban areas with good public transportation systems and few policy restrictions on movement between institutions, students move freely among two- and four-year institutions, depending upon course availability and convenience.

A second major variable is state and institutional policies. Some universities in our study, following a policy described candidly by their faculty as "academic protectionism," limited the courses that they would accept for other than elective credit and prohibited matriculated students from earning additional credits at a community college even when students had transferred with fewer than the sixty hours generally permitted under articulation agreements. Policies also influenced the number of hours completed before transferring. Students completed the greatest number of hours before transferring in states where the associate degree was given special status or where universities were prohibited from requiring transfer students to repeat core courses.

Finally, course availability was an important consideration. Community colleges that did not offer advanced courses regularly and at convenient times encouraged their students to transfer early. Asian students, for example, are the most likely to transfer early, partly because of the paucity of advanced science and math courses in community colleges.

Several studies illustrate the influence of these variables on transfer rates and timing. The Maryland State Board for Community Colleges (1983) reported that 32 percent of those entering its institutions in the fall of 1978 identified transfer as their primary objective. Five years later 64 percent of those with this goal reported its achievement. As often happens, minority students were underrepresented among respondents to the survey (17 percent) in comparison with their representation in the study population (26 percent). When the transfer of students who did not have a baccalaureate as their original objective is counted, the actual proportion of those transferring probably did not exceed 30 percent. But these are statewide averages; suburban colleges transfer a higher proportion of their students and urban institutions correspondingly fewer students. And Maryland, unlike some other states, has maintained a strong emphasis on the transfer function within a relatively free-market postsecondary environment.

SUNY has increased the number of students transferring from two-year to four-year colleges within the system during a period when overall enrollments in SUNY and transfers from non-SUNY institutions have been declining. An extensive study of transfer and articulation within SUNY concluded that the most logical explanation for this phenomenon was action by the board of trustees in 1980 that reaffirmed and strengthened the transfer policy. Board action was followed by a number of studies, reports, and recommendations leading to institutional compacts and other actions that improved opportunities for student transfer (Lavin, 1986). Interestingly, the reform of general education currently under way among both two- and four-year colleges in New York State threatens to undo much of the progress of the last five years and thus demonstrates anew the continuing propensity of the transfer process for mischief. So once again the SUNY board is addressing articulation and transfer issues as a priority.

While the overall trend in numbers of transfer students from California community colleges remains downward, some institutions have managed to reverse the trend by establishing exemplary articulation programs. Sacramento City College, which serves a high proportion of minority students, has increased its minority transfers to the University of California, Davis, by 34 percent, while a sister college in the same district serving a lower proportion of minority students has experienced a 14 percent decline in its transfers to UC Davis. The existence of a transfer articulation program funded by the Ford Foundation at Sacramento City College appears to have made a critical difference. Other districts in California have also bucked the trend through such special interventions as the state-funded transfer centers. But the trend remains downward, and inner-city colleges such as those in the Los Angeles and Peralta districts are contributing disproportionately to the decline (California Postsecondary Education Commission, 1986).

But caution must be exercised in interpreting comparisons between SUNY and California colleges. In SUNY, the number of full-time students who transferred from a two-year to a four-year college in 1984 was 5,203 (Lavin, 1986). By contrast, in the same year 5,257 community college students transferred to the University of California system, while an additional 45,476 transferred to the California State University system (California Postsecondary Education Commission, 1986). Clearly transfer, even at a diminished rate, is a much larger part of the state plan for providing educational opportunities in California than in New York. While the differences in policy approaches have a significant impact on the number of students who transfer, in both systems a combination of board actions and institutional initiatives has improved transfer opportunities for all students, with minority students benefiting disproportionately.

In California, the master plan limits enrollment in the University of California (UC) to the top one-eighth of the high school graduating classes and in the California State University (CSU) to the top one-third. As a result, community colleges enroll 40 percent of all California high school graduates but 80 percent of all minority high school graduates. A report from the state chancellor's office (California Community Colleges, 1984), while declaring the determination of a transfer rate impossible, offered the following insights (p. 35):

> Younger students enrolled full time at a community college are three times as likely to transfer as older students enrolled part time.
>
> Comparing the number who transfer with total community college enrollment (which produces the low estimates in the 3 to 5 percent range) is not valid. The most appropriate comparison is with the first-time, full-time less than twenty-five year olds.
>
> Nearly half of this group transfers to CSU or UC two years after entrance. An additional one in ten will transfer during the same period to an independent four-year institution.

A recent report of the Educational Equity Advisory Council of CSU provides additional information on minority access in California (California State University, 1986, p. 7):

> CSU is failing to attract Hispanics and blacks into freshman classes in percentages commensurate with their high school graduation rates.
>
> Over two-thirds of new black admits and one-half of new Hispanic admits do not meet regular admission criteria.

> New community college transfer rates for blacks and Hispanics are somewhat below their respective high school graduation rates.
>
> Five-year graduation rates for blacks and Hispanics, whether admitted through regular or special processes, are substantially lower than such rates for Asian and white students.

The California experience, while skewed in the direction of greater reliance on transfer as the major access strategy by the state's master plan, parallels the experience of other states. Universities report that minority students are seriously underrepresented in their freshman classes. A high proportion of the blacks and Hispanics who enter as freshmen do not meet regular admission requirements. The attrition rates for blacks and Hispanics entering as freshmen reflect the fact that large numbers of them are underprepared according to regular admission standards.

Blacks and Hispanics experience higher attrition rates in community college transfer programs than do Asians and whites. And they are less well represented in university transfer student populations than among entering freshmen. Universities typically place their recruiting emphasis on the more academically rigorous suburban colleges. As a result, the proportions of blacks and Hispanics among transfer students at the junior level often fail to equal the proportions of these groups among first-time freshmen at the same universities. Once admitted as juniors, minority students do not persist in ways significantly different from those of nonminorities, although they do on the average earn significantly lower grade point averages. Within universities, minority students admitted as freshmen without meeting prescribed admission requirements and transfer students admitted from predominantly minority inner-city colleges appear to be at particular risk.

Most students who transfer do so after completing close to the equivalent of two years of study at a community college. Fifty-four percent of the transfer students responding to our survey held the associate degree when they transferred. White and Asian students were the least likely to have the degree. The average number of hours earned before transferring for community college students attending the University of Missouri, St. Louis, was over fifty. In Arizona, for every student who transferred to Arizona State University after completing one academic year in a community college, eight transferred after completing two years. Eighty-two percent of the new undergraduate transfers at the University of Illinois, Chicago, were classified as sophomores or above.

While high proportions of the students attending inner-city colleges are underprepared for traditional academic work, at least 5 percent of those who carry six or more credit hours per semester represent potential transfer students in terms of their aspirations and behavior. Among those who do transfer, one-fourth to one-third subsequently earn the baccalaureate degree within three to five years. One in twenty may not sound like a large percentage, but when it is applied to the significant number of minority students enrolled in urban institutions, the potential impact of changes in the rate of transfer or retention on discrepancies between minority and nonminority degree achievement becomes substantial.

Performance of Transfer Students

As with transfer behavior, at least three major variables influence the performance of transfer students at receiving institutions. First, there are clear differences that can be attributed to the majors that they choose. At Arizona State University, students transferring into the colleges of business, engineering, and fine arts experienced an average grade point loss of .56. By contrast, those transferring into the liberal arts lost .35 grade points (Richardson and Doucette, 1980).

A second important variable involves the community college from which a student transfers. One university that had studied the phenomenon over a seven-year period reported that the grade point averages of black students who transferred from predominantly inner-city colleges averaged a full grade point below those of their nonminority counterparts. A second university reported grade point losses ranging from 1.05 to 1.28 for students transferring from predominantly minority institutions in their service area. These losses contrasted with a drop of .37 for students from a better integrated community college in the same district. Perhaps even more discouraging than the wide disparity in student performance among community colleges within the same districts was the lack of interest among some district administrative personnel in obtaining and using such information to improve educational practice.

The conclusion that segregation in urban community colleges promotes the same discrepancies in student performance as segregation in urban public schools seems inescapable. In a related study being conducted by the senior author of this work, a highly selective campus of the University of California reported that it received few if any transfer students from predominantly minority community colleges. Minority students who transferred or entered as native freshmen were increasingly middle class and came from suburban schools or colleges with predominantly white populations. Significantly, California has removed restrictions on attendance at community colleges outside the district in which a student resides. As a result, the better prepared and more highly motivated minority students increasingly attend integrated community colleges in suburban areas, a phenomenon that we also noted in other states. This voluntary migration to higher-quality community colleges solves problems for individual students, but does nothing to widen opportunities for those who remain in the inner city.

A third variable influencing student performance after transfer relates to the competitiveness of the university that a student attends. Within California, students transferring into the state university system experienced a first-semester grade point loss of .27. Those entering the more competitive University of California system lost .57 (California Community Colleges, 1984). In Texas as in California, the more competitive universities require transfer students to have a grade point average of .5 to 1.0 higher than the grade point average they require of their native students for good standing in the same programs. Such practices are often cited by community college leaders as discriminatory, but the university considers them necessary to prevent excessive attrition among transfer students.

The problem of competition in the transfer institution is intensified for community colleges serving high proportions of minority students. The *Chicago Study of Access and Choice in Higher Education* (Orfield and others, 1984) concluded that predominantly minority community colleges were significantly less successful in transferring students than were integrated or predominantly white community colleges. Students who transferred from predominantly minority community colleges were most likely to transfer to predominantly minority four-year institutions, where the career choices and academic expectations were more attenuated than at their better integrated sister universities. Those students in our survey who transferred to a predominantly white university were significantly more critical of their preparation than were their counterparts from the same predominantly minority community college who transferred to a predominantly minority university.

Raising questions about the performance of graduates of predominantly minority community colleges is sometimes criticized as "blaming the victim for the crime." But from our perspective it is not the victim who emerges as the culprit in this analysis but rather the system that accepts segregation in postsecondary institutions while making every effort to remove it from the public schools.

Reliance on aggregate data produces the comfortable conclusion that community college transfer students continue to perform as well in universities as they have for the past twenty years. Following an initial "shock," which is reflected in the loss of approximately .5 grade points from their community college averages, they settle down and graduate at rates equal to, or in some instances better than, their native university student counterparts. But aggregate figures can be deceptive. Many suburban community colleges have maintained strong academic programs, and they are able to transfer students who perform well in the most competitive universities. But the more urban community colleges attended disproportionately by minority students present a very different picture. In these colleges vocational emphasis reduces opportunities for students to take the courses needed for transfer on a reasonable schedule. The flight of more capable students to colleges that have maintained better academic reputations limits competition and means that advanced courses will probably not attract sufficient enrollments to make it economically feasible to offer them. In addition, the lack of appropriate assessment and placement procedures places pressure on faculty to reduce standards.

For these reasons and because of differences in high school preparation, minority students are less well represented among transfer populations than they are in the feeder community colleges from which they come. This loss in proportional representation characterized the nonpredominantly minority community colleges in our survey. And it applies in California, where minorities represent 39 percent of the full-time enrollment in community colleges but only 28 percent of the transfers to UC and CSU (California Community Colleges, 1984). The hopeful news is that those underrepresented minority students who do transfer, while attaining lower grade point averages than their peers, nonetheless graduate at similar rates. Clearly, the urban connection between community colleges and universities can contribute to minority degree achievement in ways that are not currently being fully exploited.

Student assessment of community college preparation depends on the expectations of the institution to which they transfer. Students attending research universities were more likely to be critical of their community college preparation than those attending comprehensive institutions with a teaching focus. Students were most critical of their preparation in science and math, where advanced courses rely heavily on mastery of the content and methods of prerequisite courses.

Black and Hispanic students were the most positive about their previous experiences, which may reflect the emphasis on support and nurturing found in the community colleges that serve a predominantly minority clientele, but the majority of students thought that they were reasonably well prepared. The greatest number of their concerns focused on the problems of obtaining reliable information from counselors and the lack of specific opportunities to focus on preparation for transfer. Many students felt unprepared for the academic demands that they encountered at the university. In the academic areas, the most common concerns were lack of continuity and insufficient rigor in course offerings, along with the failure to enforce course prerequisites.

Conclusion

The questions that drove this study were designed to assess the potential contribution of articulation and transfer policies to reducing discrepancies between minority and nonminority rates for attaining the baccalaureate degree. The problem is admittedly complex. Family structure, racism in the larger society, economic status, residential patterns, and a host of other circumstances over which higher educational institutions have little, if any, control all influence prevailing patterns of achievement. The good news is that institutions in the short term can intervene with color-free strategies that improve opportunities for all students while providing a particular boost for minorities.

Transfer and articulation policies are only one piece of the larger state and institutional puzzle. To optimize outcomes, attention must also be given to expanding the pool of prepared high school graduates as well as to encouraging four-year colleges to make equal opportunity a special concern. But despite the acknowledged importance of cooperation between high schools and colleges and of the need for universities to improve their programs for minorities who enter as native freshmen, urban minorities remain disproportionately enrolled in community colleges from which they graduate and transfer in proportions well below their representation either in high school graduating classes or in their community colleges. Closer working relationships between community colleges, adjacent universities, and state coordinating boards can improve baccalaureate opportunities in urban settings, a possibility addressed in greater detail in the next chapter.

10

Helping Minorities Achieve Degrees: Recommendations for Community Colleges, Universities, and State Boards

Most underrepresented minority students either attend community colleges or enter four-year institutions as freshmen through a differentially qualified category. For the most part, they are not as well represented among transfer cohorts as they are among high school graduates or in community colleges. Moreover, those who meet regular admission requirements as freshmen in four-year institutions are not as well prepared as their nonminority counterparts because of the narrower course offerings and lower level of competition in the high schools that they typically attend. (That academic success is a function of preparation rather than of race was stated eloquently in a position paper prepared for a board of regents by the chancellor of one of the universities we visited.)

Clearly, removing barriers to effective transfer will help all students, not simply those who come from minority backgrounds. Those who prefer targeted strategies that address primarily or exclusively the issue of underrepresentation may deplore this fact. But the realities of life in a society struggling to become color blind call for strategies that can be applied on some basis other than race. The appeal of need-based financial aid, which clearly benefits minority students disproportionately, is its evenhanded application on the basis of economic circumstances. Improving articulation practices among institutions sharing the same urban settings offers a similar appeal. It will help all students, but minority students will benefit disproportionately because they live disproportionately in cities and depend disproportionately on public higher education. In addition, by working together to solve problems of student access and achievement, urban community colleges and universities can gain valuable insights into the practices that many higher education institutions will need to follow during the next decade, as ever higher proportions of their students exhibit the characteristics of students now found primarily in urban settings.

Earlier chapters focused on identifying relationships between (1) the actions of faculty, administrators, and state coordinating board officials and (2) the quality of the baccalaureate opportunities available to urban minority students who begin their postsecondary education in a community college. Our purpose was to produce an accurate description of the variables that institutions and state coordinating boards can control, thus allowing them to influence degree achievement by their students. Accurate descriptions of relevant variables within systems can do much to empower participants by making them aware of probable cause and effect relationships, thus improving the correlation between the intent of policy decisions and their probable outcomes.

In this chapter we move beyond description to suggest the implications of the data for policy decisions by institutional and state coordinating board officials. The changes recommended do not require urban universities to give up their aspirations for major research status. Nor do we recommend that community colleges give up their strong philosophical commitment to access and comprehensiveness. But we do suggest that publicly supported colleges in urban settings should show a greater willingness to view themselves as partners in pursuit of a common goal rather than competitors in pursuit of institutional enhancement. And we argue that state coordinating boards should provide the necessary incentives and regulatory influences to ensure that improved cooperation receives priority consideration by institutional personnel.

Recommendations for Community Colleges

Urban community colleges remain the most important and sometimes only avenue to upward socioeconomic mobility for large numbers of minority students in a society where being uneducated and being unemployed seem ever more closely linked. Under such circumstances, it is not difficult to understand why so much emphasis has been placed on making students employable. Even though half of the students who attend urban community colleges have the baccalaureate degree as a primary objective, fewer than half with this objective engage in the necessary transfer-related behaviors.

Inner-city students who earn the baccalaureate degree do so only after overcoming odds that to many middle-class educators appear insurmountable. Partly as a result, some administrators have concluded that the most important, if not exclusive, role of the urban community college should be to teach vocational/technical skills. This conclusion would be more defensible if urban community college districts exhibited racial balance as one of their distinctive characteristics. Unfortunately, many do not. So the decision to emphasize vocational/technical skills at inner-city colleges, however justifiable from the perspective of student preparation and efficient use of educational resources, is also a decision to deny some percentage of inner-city residents, mostly minority ones, the opportunity to escape the circumstances to which they have fallen heir as a result of where they reside.

Urban community college districts work hard to preserve access for their disadvantaged populations. Their location in areas with serious and debilitating social problems motivates them to do all they can to alleviate the human misery that they daily encounter. They help people get the jobs necessary to self-respect and family integrity. But while carrying out these important functions, can they also keep open the baccalaureate door to those who, by escaping from poverty, will be able to demonstrate to an increasingly disbelieving cohort that the system can work?

Those who lead inner-city institutions were not in agreement about the answer to this question. At one extreme, faculty and administrators in one of the colleges in our study felt the transfer function to be of minor importance because of the need to prepare students for immediate employment. In a similar vein, faculty advisers at a different college counseled transfer-bound students to leave as soon as possible because they did not believe it was in the student's interests to remain any longer than necessary at the community college. At the other end of the continuum, an urban college described the academic transfer function as the cornerstone of its mission. As a result, admissions and academic placement procedures reflected a concern with program planning, support services, ongoing monitoring of progress, and carefully structured learning experiences, all of which were designed to encourage as many students as possible to aspire to the baccalaureate without limiting opportunities to prepare for employment for those who chose that alternative.

Transfer opportunities do not need to be an either/or proposition. Inner-city colleges frequently are situated in areas of high unemployment. Their students are among the least mobile in our society. Providing entry-level employment skills as well as opportunities for upgrading for those who already have jobs will remain an important responsibility for community colleges, but ways must be found to provide access to the baccalaureate as well. A number of strategies, attainable for most inner-city colleges within current budget constraints, would help to preserve some reasonable balance for their students between the demands of the present and dreams of the future. Community colleges should work to achieve a high degree of continuity between their transfer programs and related programs in the four-year institutions to which their students most commonly transfer. Some of the actions that would contribute the most to attaining this objective include

1. maintaining a full range of transfer courses scheduled according to some preannounced and guaranteed timetable.

While it might not be economically feasible to offer every course every semester, on both a day and evening basis, it should be possible for students to complete lower-division requirements on the campus of primary attendance without unreasonable delays.

2. offering transfer courses for the same number of credit hours as major receiving institutions and making certain that the content of these courses is parallel
3. awarding associate degrees in arts or sciences for the completion of any approved lower-division sequence of a four-year college or university to which students regularly transfer without the necessity of taking courses unique to the community college
4. offering incentives for students to graduate with associate degrees where programs lead to full junior status after transfer

There is also a need to balance the emphasis on access and responsiveness to the community with an equal emphasis on effectiveness and quality control. Quality in education and access to it are not mutually exclusive goals, but quality does require a reasonable relationship between available resources and breadth of activity. Actions needed to reassure four-year institutions and the general public about the community college concern for quality include

1. limiting entrance to all transfer courses to students who demonstrate appropriate preparation in reading, writing, and math skills so that courses are comparable in difficulty to the baccalaureate offerings of major receiving institutions
2. assessing all entering students interested in enrolling in any transfer offering to ensure that they possess the requisite skills
3. requiring mandatory placement in remedial courses for any students whose assessments reveal deficiencies
4. permitting students who are placed initially in remedial courses to exit to transfer offerings only after demonstrating that they have remedied the deficiencies that led to their initial placement

5. strengthening course rigor by placing greater emphasis on reading for comprehension and writing to synthesize, as contrasted with reading for recognition and multiple-choice examinations to test recognition
6. revising course requirements and grading practices in university-parallel courses to make them more comparable to those that the students will experience after transferring
7. reassessing the rationale for offering the associate degree in general education. If the reassessment leads to the conclusion that the degree remains primarily an award for attendance, a mechanism for keeping students without educational plans eligible for financial aid, or a public relations device to provide the appearance of program completion, the degree should be replaced by some alternative less confusing to students and to the general public.
8. offering stronger liberal arts programs along with opportunities for honors work to enhance the image of the community college as a place where serious students can find a challenge. Colleges serving the urban poor in particular should not relinquish the time-honored goal of producing broadly educated men and women in favor of producing technicians.

Community colleges should also increase their emphasis on program continuity and achievement without relinquishing the caring attitudes that have been their hallmark. Students who are the first in their families to attempt higher education require special support and understanding if the opportunity extended to them is to be meaningful. But the special support should be provided in an environment that stresses achievement rather than in one that makes exceptions or excuses for these students. Practices that would contribute to this objective include

1. establishing integration as a priority objective. Facilitating attendance across district boundaries and providing free transportation between sites currently characterized by racial imbalance represent potential strategies for addressing this priority.

2. balancing the use of technology to individualize instruction with such human interventions as tutoring to ensure that students develop emotionally and socially while simultaneously mastering new competencies
3. continuing the excellent progress already made in employing minority administrators and faculty members
4. establishing realistic standards of progress and helping students achieve those standards through carefully structured monitoring procedures. Students who do not meet established standards after reasonable trial periods should be counseled to withdraw promptly to conserve institutional resources for those who are making progress.
5. emphasizing motivational activities that promote social, cultural, and physical development
6. helping students develop the coping skills required in the more impersonal environment of the receiving university
7. employing as many full-time faculty as resources will permit and providing them with released time for activities essential to students' informational needs or overall development

Comprehensive and reliable information should be provided to community college students as early as possible in their college careers. Students who have few reliable alternative sources of information about college require help in assessing their strengths and weaknesses as these apply to the costs and benefits of attaining a college degree. Most of all, they need assistance in developing realistic educational plans that neither overlook their deficiencies nor place too much emphasis on them. Throughout this study, we found that no intervention was more important than providing information in a timely fashion. Actions that would improve the flow of information to students attending urban community colleges include

1. identifying potential transfer students as early as possible and providing them with accurate information about baccalaureate opportunities and requirements
2. entering into consortium arrangements with major receiving

institutions to maintain eligibility for financial aid for students completing the transition between the two institutions

3. improving faculty advising and counseling to help students accomplish transfer without loss of course credits. Emphasis on maintaining current information among counseling staffs appears particularly essential.
4. strengthening orientation programs as a means for coordinating assessment, advising transfer students, and disseminating information

Finally, community colleges need to enter into arrangements with the four-year institutions to which their students commonly transfer, as well as with the high schools from which their students most frequently come. Such arrangements could be a means of helping students cope with the transition to the distinctive cultures of two- and four-year colleges. Actions that will improve relationships between two- and four-year institutions or improve the qualifications of high school graduates include

1. participating in joint programs with university and high school faculty to define desired educational outcomes and to develop strategies for achieving them. Particularly desirable are activities that involve joint teaching or the joint production of educational materials. The exchange of representatives on key committees related to the curriculum would also be helpful.
2. encouraging universities to offer transitional courses on the community college campus for credit
3. involving university and community college faculty in summer transitional programs that provide opportunities for minority students to strengthen academic skills
4. providing educationally disadvantaged students with an attractive and challenging alternative to the last three years of high school as is done in middle-college programs of the type offered by LaGuardia Community College under joint sponsorship of the college and the board of education

5. inviting university student service workers to spend blocks of time on a community college campus, as is the practice in the transfer centers program in California
6. encouraging junior and senior high school students to visit the campus to reduce their apprehensions about their ability to cope with the physical environment. Such visits should also be used to encourage students to do more early planning for college attendance.

Recommendations for Urban Universities

The Carnegie Commission in 1972 recommended that community colleges should have major responsibility for increasing access to higher education, with comprehensive colleges taking the lead in expanding access to upper-division work. These recommendations appear to have been implemented, but there are reasons to be concerned about the degree of equity that has resulted.

Comprehensive universities are more concerned than research universities about their teaching responsibilities and the social milieu in which they function. They also serve high proportions of minority students, employ more minority administrators and faculty members, report more concern about underprepared students and more programs to assist them, and, with rare exceptions, work more closely with community colleges that serve high proportions of minority students. But comprehensive universities also report many of the same problems that constrain research universities in their efforts to serve minority students. Programs for the underprepared are not well integrated with mainstream activities, faculty involvement is very limited, support services lack measurable goals and standards, evaluation of special programs is largely descriptive, and programs effective in retaining minority students are poorly articulated with discipline-based programs (California State University, 1986).

As a further complication to the Carnegie Commission recommendations, comprehensive universities are not available in some cities, and in others they are much less conveniently located than the research university. Further, they do not offer the same range of programs, and many of the most desired majors are located exclusively in the research institutions. In several cities where there are both comprehensive universities and research universities, the comprehensive institutions enroll a heavily minority student population and have reputations for less rigor and lower quality than the research institutions. Comprehensive universities, including those that enroll predominantly minority student bodies, certainly make important contributions to the achievement of national and state access and equity goals. Still, it is difficult to believe that significant improvement to the current maldistribution of educational opportunities will come from a system that largely relieves urban research universities of their responsibility for reducing discrepancies between the achievement of minority and nonminority students.

Thus, while most research universities may accept their responsibility for improving degree opportunities for minorities, there remain important disjunctures between the acknowledgment of this responsibility and the response to it. Many problems result from forces outside internal university decision processes, but some are amenable to institutional intervention. Urban universities can strengthen working relationships with community colleges that enroll significant numbers of minority students. California's transfer centers and the UCLA Transfer Alliance Program are examples of this concept. Other actions that would contribute to the achievement of this objective are

1. holding regular articulation meetings between administrators in related service areas, including financial aid, records, counseling, and admissions
2. providing systematic feedback on the performance, persistence, and graduation rates of transfer students disaggregated by race
3. giving community colleges early notification of impending catalogue changes

There is also need to improve the continuity experienced by students when moving from a community college to an adjacent university. Among the steps that would enhance continuity are

1. coordinating academic calendars and credits in comparable courses
2. providing the same catalogue guarantees to community college transfers as to native students
3. encouraging university faculty members to become better acquainted with the problems faced by inner-city community colleges and public school systems
4. helping community college faculty members improve their understanding of the content and methodologies of upper-division courses for which their community college courses serve as prerequisites
5. offering special opportunities for community college counselors to become better informed about university requirements and procedures

Barrier-free transition from adjacent community colleges should be established by universities as a planning priority. The following areas in particular should receive consideration:

1. targeting a reasonable part of the total admissions effort on community colleges that enroll high proportions of minority students
2. arranging for faculty representatives from major receiving programs to visit related community college classes to improve the quality of information available to prospective transfer students
3. developing an office responsible for program planning for transfer students to provide advising before and after transfer
4. strengthening orientation programs for transfer students and making them an attractive part of the registration process through such strategies as providing priority in course selection

Universities should work to improve the environment for

minority student achievement. Actions that have potential for moderating students' perceptions that the university represents a hostile or racist environment include

1. sensitizing faculty and administrators to the problems confronting minority students by employing more qualified minority faculty members and administrators
2. integrating special support services for minority students and those who staff them into the mainstream of university activity
3. publicizing the university commitment to minority student achievement through targeted financial assistance and guarantees of continuing support for categorically funded programs of demonstrated effectiveness
4. conducting and publicizing needs assessments in such areas as residence halls, child care, parking, and security. Needs identified should receive priority in university resource allocation procedures.
5. improving opportunities for minority students to feel that their culture is represented and respected on campus. In major part this is a function of campus presence. Faculty members respect minority cultures most in those institutions where enough minority students are enrolled to constitute visible evidence of their importance to the future well-being of the university. And students feel more at home in institutions where they see members of their own race in key administrative and faculty roles.
6. developing cohesive, cooperative learning groups among new minority transfer students through block scheduling in courses and through residence hall assignments

The educational practices of universities should communicate clearly their expectations for community college transfer students and should provide support and assistance to community colleges and their students in meeting such expectations. Some practices that would contribute to these objectives are

1. offering junior-level transition classes taught by university faculty members on community college campuses

2. defining competencies expected of upper-division students and working cooperatively with community college staff to identify and implement appropriate assessment procedures
3. redesigning the transcript evaluation process so that transfer students are provided with a single estimate of the credits that the university will recognize in relation to a stated program choice
4. encouraging students who choose or who are required to attend a community college as their point of entry to higher education to earn an associate in arts or science degree before transferring unless they plan to major in a field where this is not feasible
5. accepting community college students who do not initially meet university admission standards only after they have completed with satisfactory grades a prescribed sequence of not fewer than twenty-four semester hours, including courses in composition, math, and the sciences
6. providing summer transition programs for transfer students similar to those offered for high school seniors

Universities also face pressures to adapt current practices that are designed around the needs of full-time day students. A growing number of part-time, working adults are reaching upper-division status after studying for the equivalent of two years at a community college. Among this population are many black students who tend to be older and to have more family responsibilities than other students. Several university studies indicated that this group was overrepresented among those who dropped out. Part of the reason attrition rates were so high among all part-time students, but among minorities in particular, involved their preference for studying in the evening. But universities offered courses rather than programs in the evening, and many of the most desired majors could not be completed without attending at least some day classes. Services for evening students were limited. In these and other ways, universities communicated the lack of priority they attached to those who could not devote full time to their studies. If universities are to escape the loss of program coherence and continuity earlier experienced by community colleges in responding to pressures from these same part-time students, planning for evening services and program offerings must receive high priority.

Recommendations for State Coordinating Boards

The role of coordinating boards varies along a continuum from bureaucratic and reactive to issue oriented and proactive. Some differences can be attributed to the powers assigned by state legislation. Others appear to devolve from planning capabilities and the preferences of staff. But all boards have in common the responsibilities for maintaining system integrity and the need to balance institutional interests against the priorities and concerns of those whom the system was designed to serve.

Improving opportunities for minority students to earn bachelor's degrees from a state coordinating board perspective involves encouraging institutions to give greater attention to their responsibilities as part of a system, a proposition against which most find it difficult to argue. In fact, the extent to which improved articulation equates with apple pie and motherhood is part of the problem. Because no one wants to be characterized as opposed to policies that obviously serve the public interest, everyone favors quality in education, academic freedom, and institutional integrity. Regrettably, there is a very thin line between the appropriate use of these concepts in defense of the academic enterprise and their inappropriate use to pursue narrow institutional interests. The strategies described below have been implemented by one or more states without apparent adverse effects on the quality or integrity of the institutions to which they have been applied.

To begin with, state coordinating boards should establish clear expectations that publicly funded two- and four-year institutions will, as a priority, work closely together to provide opportunities for trouble-free transfer. This objective can be promoted through defining institutional missions in ways that limit competition and through establishing explicit responsibilities for cooperation. Admission standards and responsibilities for remediation represent areas that should receive special attention in revised mission statements.

State coordinating boards should also work to achieve common academic calendars among all publicly funded institutions within their respective states. The decision by any institution to follow a quarter system as distinct from a semester system is a matter of historical accident rather than of compelling logic. Once established and sanctified by information systems and course outlines, however, the decision takes on a life of its own. It is neither easy nor inexpensive to convert from one system to the other. Nevertheless, differences in academic calendars represent an important source of difficulty for transfer students and one of the least problematic to remedy from the state perspective, provided that institutions involved in the conversion receive appropriate consideration in their budgets.

The associate degree in arts or science should be defined as the preferred credential for transfer. Students earning one of these degrees in an approved major should be guaranteed junior status at any public university in the state, subject only to space limitations. This approach seems far more conducive to trouble-free transfer than articulation on a course-by-course basis or designing core areas for majors. States should give serious consideration to adopting this recommendation in conjunction with some form of competency exam that would be administered to all students seeking status as upper-division undergraduates.

There may be some majors—architecture and fine arts for example—where having taken lower-division courses at a community college may work to the disadvantage of a student. Such majors should be clearly identified in the transfer literature of both two- and four-year colleges. Further, the burden of proof for excluding any major should be placed on the university requesting the exemption. Community colleges should be required to redefine their transfer associate degrees as noted above to ensure that students are no longer required to choose between meeting the requirements for a community college degree and fulfilling the lower-division program of studies specified for a baccalaureate major.

Each state should consider establishing an articulation coordinating committee. Membership would include representatives from public and private two- and four-year colleges and from the state coordinating board. Depending on the scope of committee responsibility, it may also prove valuable to include representatives from the kindergarten-through-grade-12 sector. As a minimum, committee responsibilities should include

1. overseeing the transfer process to include responsibility for defining articulation issues and advancing recommendations for their resolution to institutional governing boards and to the state coordinating board
2. monitoring the continuity of academic programs and related institutional practices designed to facilitate transfer
3. serving as an appeal board for students whose concerns about the award of transfer credit or other aspects of the transfer process are not satisfied through the normal institutional grievance procedures
4. appointing working subcommittees comprised of appropriate institutional representatives to study articulation issues and to recommend solutions to problems
5. obtaining access to institutional data necessary to the conduct of committee business

State coordinating boards should create a common framework for numbering and titling courses intended to meet lower-division requirements for a baccalaureate degree. This framework, while stopping short of the common course numbering system employed in one of the study states, could set forth the following expectations:

1. The same band of numbers would be used by all public institutions in identifying freshman and sophomore courses applicable to the bachelor's degree.
2. Only those courses clearly acceptable for baccalaureate credit by the state's public four-year institutions would be assigned to the specified band of numbers by community colleges.
3. Course titles and course descriptions would be as similar as possible across institutions.
4. Courses designed to meet comparable lower-division gen-

eral education requirements would carry the same number of credit hours at universities and community colleges.

Public universities and community colleges should be encouraged to share information necessary for efficient operation of the transfer process and for monitoring the effectiveness of student preparation. At a minimum, the following guidelines should be enacted:

1. Student-specific data providing information on the performance of transfers should be provided to community colleges by their major receiving universities on at least an annual basis. Data should be disaggregated by race and number of hours completed before transfer.
2. Where the volume of student transfer is large, institutions should be encouraged to explore the electronic exchange of transcript information.
3. Catalogue requirements in effect the year that a student matriculates as a freshman should be applied to community college transfers in the same manner as to native students.
4. Universities should be encouraged to maintain a student advisement manual or brochure for each group of related majors that receives a significant number of transfer students.

The policies governing the administration of student financial aid programs should provide the same continuity of coverage for transfer students as for those who begin in universities. In particular, attention should be given to the information and transition problems experienced by students whose eligibility for state financial aid changes significantly as a result of moving from a lower-cost two-year college to a more expensive public or private four-year institution. States should also consider providing special incentives for the joint use of facilities by community colleges and the universities to which most of their students transfer. For example, community colleges might offer remedial courses to the more marginally prepared university students on the campus of the university. Universities might offer selected junior-level courses on a community college campus to provide a transition experience.

Conclusion

Institutional efforts are only one part of the equation for improved equity. Statewide governing and coordinating boards have an equally important role to play. All the strategies described in this chapter can be found in some form or other among the states visited during the preparation of this volume. In most instances they are not employed systematically, however, and conflicting practices or behaviors lead to their attenuation. Only statewide boards have the scope and authority to foster the necessary combination of moral leadership, consistency and predictability in institutional practice, adequate resource allocation, and systemwide monitoring for accountability.

The results are evident in states where this combination has been put to work. In California, several community colleges and universities have taken advantage of state and foundation incentives to reverse the downward trend among minority student transfers to some of the most selective universities in the world. In New York, a combination of governing board leadership and institutional initiatives has increased the flow of students from community colleges to senior institutions when all available demographic data would predict the opposite outcome.

New Jersey has established, during a period of intensive competition for a declining number of high school graduates, a sophisticated and powerful student assessment program in which both public and independent institutions participate. The program provides agreed-upon and measurable competencies for enrollment in college-level course work. All types of institutions share in the responsibility for remediation so that improvements in student preparation will not be purchased at the expense of decreasing minority representation in four-year institutions.

Tennessee has been recognized nationally for linking resource allocation to institutional performance along quality dimensions. One of the important quality indicators that Tennessee rewards is student progress, which encompasses the retention and graduation of minority students. The Tennessee State Board of Regents has taken a systematic approach to improving quality and access—an approach that includes evaluating system administrators on their progress in meeting affirmative action goals. The results of this approach are evident at Memphis State, where participation and graduation rates for minority students are very nearly equivalent in a majority of the institution's programs.

Specific approaches vary as a consequence of state context and political history. But the results are positive in those states that have implemented comprehensive and systematic programs aimed at improving both quality of education and access to it. Conversely, the worst results occur in states where boards provide laissez-faire leadership and institutions rely on special equity programs rather than making access and quality everyone's business. The opportunity for improvement is present in every state. All that is needed are leadership and commitment.

Appendix

Transferring from Community College to University

A Survey to Improve Opportunities for Students

1. Please list the community college where you earned *most* of your credits before transferring, the number of terms attended, and the credit hours earned:

   College name ____________________

   Terms attended ____________ Credit hours earned ____________

2. How many of the credit hours earned at the community college identified above:

   Were accepted by your university? ________

   Will count toward the bachelor's degree? ________

3. What was your average grade in the community college identified above? (Mark one)

   A ☐ *B* ☐ *C* ☐ *D* ☐

4. Compared to the grades I earned at community college, my university grades are: (Mark one)

   Higher ☐ The same ☐ Lower ☐ No term completed ☐

5. When did you first decide to transfer to a university? (Mark one)

   Before starting classes at the community college ☐

   During attendance at the community college ☐

   After leaving the community college ☐

6. How important was each of the following in your decision to attend this university? (Mark one answer for each)

	Very Important	*Somewhat Important*	*Not Important*
Advice of a community college teacher			
Advice of a community college counselor			
Advice of a friend or relative			
Number of credit hours accepted			
It is close to where I live			
University has good academic reputation			
The program I wanted was available			
Financial assistance was offered			
Information from university representative			
Recruited by athletic department			
Reputation of the university for social activities			
Low tuition			
Family responsibilities or a job made it impossible to go away to school			
This university's graduates get good jobs			
This university's graduates get admitted to good graduate and professional schools			

7. Below are listed some of the sources of information and assistance for students who transfer. How useful were each of these sources for you? (Mark one answer for each source)

Community College Sources	*Very Useful*	*Somewhat Useful*	*Not Useful*	*Not Used*
Counseling office				
Teachers				

Community College Sources	*Very Useful*	*Somewhat Useful*	*Not Useful*	*Not Used*
Orientation sessions				
Registrar's office				
Financial aid office				
Honors program				
Transfer guides				
College catalogue				
Special programs for transfers				
Friends who have transferred				
University Sources Admissions office				
Teachers				
Orientation sessions				
University representatives				
Athletic representatives				
Visit to university				
Financial aid office				
University catalogue				
Other university publications				
Academic departments				
Special programs for transfers				
Special programs				

8. Below are some requirements related to classroom performance. How well did your course work *in the community college* prepare you for these requirements in university courses. (Mark one answer for each skill)

	Very Well	*Fairly Well*	*Poorly*	*Not Needed in Univ. Courses*
Writing assignments (term papers, reports)				
Computer use				
Reading assignments (textbook and other assigned work)				

	Very Well	*Fairly Well*	*Poorly*	*Not Needed in Univ. Courses*
Examinations				
Taking notes on lectures				
Classroom discussion				
Laboratory assignments				

9. How would you compare instructors, support services, and courses of the community college with those at the university in the following areas: (Mark one answer for each area)

Instructors	*Better at Comm. Coll.*	*About the Same*	*Better at Univ.*	*No Basis for Comp.*
Knowledge of material				
Organization of courses				
Capability to teach/explain course material				
Openness to student ideas				
Availability to meet with students				
Helpfulness with career plans				
Support Services/Activities				
Tutoring				
Counseling services				
Library				
Admissions procedures				
New student orientation				
Financial assistance				
Student center/union				
Cultural opportunities				
Social events				
Courses				
Offered at convenient hours				
Availability of required courses				

Courses	*Better at Comm. Coll.*	*About the Same*	*Better at Univ.*	*No Basis for Comp.*
Ease of registering/changing courses				
Relevance to your educational/ employment goals				
Appropriate level of difficulty				

10. How well did your elementary and secondary schools prepare you for university requirements in each of the following areas? (Mark one for each area)

	Very Well	*Fairly Well*	*Poorly*
Reading			
Writing			
Speaking			
Mathematics			
Science			
Social studies			

11. In which of the following fields are you planning to earn your baccalaureate degree? (Mark one)

☐ Allied health
☐ Arts or humanities
☐ Biological sciences
☐ Business or accounting
☐ Computer science
☐ Education or human services
☐ Engineering, architecture, or related technologies
☐ Physical science
☐ Mathematics
☐ Social sciences
Other (please specify) ____________________

12. Did you select the courses you took in your community college to achieve the degree identified above?

Yes ☐ No ☐

13. If you answered "No" to question #12, what was the objective that guided selection of your community college courses?

____

____

14. What is the highest level of formal education obtained by your parents? (Mark one in each column)

	Father	*Mother*
Grammar school or less		
Some high school		
High school graduate		
Some college credit		
Certificate or diploma		
Associate degree		
Bachelor's degree		
Some graduate school		
Graduate degree		

15. On the average, how many hours per week do you work outside the home for pay while attending your university? __________

16. Indicate the number of credit hours you attempted *during your first term at your university.* __________

    Of these, how many did you complete with a passing grade? ______

17. How are you currently classified by the university you attend? (Mark one)

    Freshman ☐ Sophomore ☐ Junior ☐ Senior ☐

18. How old will you be on December 31, 1985? (Mark one)

    22 or younger ☐ 23–35 ☐ 36–45 ☐ Over 45 ☐

19. Indicate the degrees or certificates you have already earned and the year for each. (Mark those applicable)

Degrees or Certificates	*Earned*	*Year*
Passed GED Test		
High school diploma		
Associate degree		
Other (please describe)		

20. Do you have dependent children who live at home with you?

    Yes ☐ No ☐ How many? __________

21. How important are each of the following financial resources in helping you meet the costs (tuition, fees, living expenses, transportation, books) of attending university? (Mark one answer for each possible source)

Financial Resources	*Very Important*	*Somewhat Important*	*Not Important*	*Not Available*
Work and savings				
Financial aid (grants and scholarships)				
Loans				
Parents or spouse				
Veteran's benefits				
Other				

22. How do you identify your ethnic status? (Mark one)

☐ American Indian/Alaskan
☐ Caucasian
☐ Hispanic
☐ Black/Afro-American
☐ Asian/Pacific Islander
Other ______________

23. Was English the language ordinarily spoken in your home when you were growing up? (Mark one)

Yes ☐ No ☐

24. Your sex (Mark one)

Male ☐ Female ☐

25. Finally, we would like to ask if you have any specific suggestions for ways of improving transfer opportunities for students such as yourself.

____
____
____
____
____
____

Thank you for your participation in this project. Please return in envelope provided.

References

American Association of State Colleges and Universities. *Connections: Urban College and University Network.* Washington, D.C.: American Association of State Colleges and Universities, 1979.

Astin, A. W. *Minorities in American Higher Education: Recent Trends, Current Prospects, and Recommendations.* San Francisco: Jossey-Bass, 1982.

Avakian, A. N., MacKinney, A. C., and Allen, G. R. "Longitudinal Study of Student Retention at an Urban University." Unpublished paper. University of Missouri, St. Louis, 1983.

Bender, L. W., and Chalfant-Thomas, S. *Achievement of the Baccalaureate: Florida Policies and Practices in Selected Areas.* Tallahassee, Fla.: Florida State University Press, 1986.

Blackwell, J. E. "Demographics of Desegregation." In R. Wilson (ed.), *Race and Equity in Higher Education.* Washington, D.C.: American Council on Education, 1982.

Borough of Manhattan Community College. *Analysis of Academic Performance After Seven Calendar Semesters for First-Time Freshmen and Advanced Standing Students Admitted in the Fall of 1979 Semester.* New York: City University of New York, 1983.

Breneman, D. W., and Nelson, S. C. *Financing Community Colleges: An Economic Perspective.* Washington, D.C.: Brookings Institution, 1981.

Cafferty, P.S.J., and Spangenberg, G. *Backs Against the Wall: Urban-Oriented Colleges and Universities and the Urban Poor and Disadvantaged.* New York: Ford Foundation, 1981.

California Community Colleges. *Transfer Education.* Sacramento, Calif.: State Chancellor's Office, 1984.

California Postsecondary Education Commission. *Update of Community College Transfer Student Statistics.* Sacramento, Calif.: California Postsecondary Education Commission, 1986.

California State University. *Educational Equity in the California State University—Which Way the Future?* Long Beach, Calif.: Office of the Chancellor, 1986.

Carnegie Commission on Higher Education. *The Campus and the City.* New York: McGraw-Hill, 1972.

Carroll, C. D. "Postsecondary Transitions: Entry, Persistence, Transfer, Dropout, and Completion for 1980 High School Graduates." Unpublished tabulation. Washington, D.C.: Longitudinal Studies Branch, National Center for Educational Statistics, 1985.

Center for the Study of Community Colleges. *Transfer Education in American Community Colleges.* Los Angeles: Ford Foundation, 1985.

Cohen, A. M., and Brawer, F. B. *The American Community College.* San Francisco: Jossey-Bass, 1982.

College Entrance Examination Board. *Student Aid and the Urban Poor.* New York: Ford Foundation, 1981.

College Entrance Examination Board. *Equality and Excellence.* New York: College Entrance Examination Board, 1985.

Davila, E. M. *Today's Urban University Students.* Part 1. New York: College Entrance Examination Board, 1985.

Desegregation Monitoring Committee. *Desegregation Progress Report.* Nashville, Tenn.: Tennessee Higher Education Commission, 1986.

Deskins, D. R., Jr. *Minority Recruitment Data.* Totowa, N.J.: Roman & Allanheld, 1983.

Evangelauf, J. "Students' Borrowing Quintuples in Decade, Raising the Specter of a 'Debtor Generation.' " *Chronicle of Higher Education.* Jan. 7, 1987, p. 1.

Fleming, J. *Blacks in College: A Comparative Study of Students' Success in Black and in White Institutions.* San Francisco: Jossey-Bass, 1984.

Florida Board of Regents. *Student Retention Within the State University System of Florida, 1983-84: Summary Findings.* Tallahassee, Fla.: State University System, Office for Equal Opportunity Programs, 1984.

Gittell, M. "A Place for Women?" In L. S. Zwerling (ed.), *The Community College and Its Critics.* New Directions for Community Colleges, no. 54. San Francisco: Jossey-Bass, 1986.

Grant, W. V., and Snyder, T. D. *Digest of Educational Statistics 1983-84.* Washington, D.C.: U.S. Government Printing Office, 1984.

Heller, S. "Reaffirm Drive for Integration, Colleges Urged." *Higher Education and National Affairs Newsletter,* Mar. 26, 1984, p. 3.

Hodgkinson, H. L. *All One System: Demographics of Education —Kindergarten Through Graduate School.* Washington, D.C.: Institute for Educational Leadership, 1985.

Jencks, C., and Riesman, D. *The Academic Revolution.* New York: Doubleday, 1968.

Karabel, J. "Community Colleges and Social Stratification in the 1980s." In L. S. Zwerling (ed.), *The Community College and Its Critics.* New Directions for Community Colleges, no. 54. San Francisco: Jossey-Bass, 1986.

Kintzer, F. C., and Wattenbarger, J. L. *The Articulation/Transfer Phenomenon: Patterns and Direction.* Horizon Issues Monograph Series. Washington, D.C.: American Association of Community and Junior Colleges, 1985.

Lavin, D. E., Murtha, J., and Kaufman, D. *Long-Term Graduation Rates of Students at City University of New York.* New York: City University of New York, 1984.

Lavin, M. W. *Current Issues in Transfer and Articulation: The*

Impact of General Education Requirements, Joint Admissions, and Services for Transfer Students. Unpublished report to SUNY. Albany, N.Y., 1986.

Maryland State Board for Community Colleges. *Four Years Later: Follow-Up of 1978 Entrance Maryland Community Colleges.* Annapolis: Maryland State Board for Community Colleges, 1983.

Millett, J. D. *Conflict in Higher Education: State Government Coordination Versus Institutional Independence.* San Francisco: Jossey-Bass, 1984.

Missouri Coordinating Board for Higher Education. *College Transfer Guidelines.* Jefferson City: Missouri Coordinating Board for Higher Education, 1984.

Murphy, J. T. *Getting the Facts: A Fieldwork Guide for Evaluations and Policy Analysts.* Glenview, Ill.: Scott, Foresman, 1980.

New Jersey Basic Skills Council. *Effectiveness of Remedial Programs in New Jersey Public Colleges and Universities.* Trenton, N.J.: Department of Higher Education, 1986.

Nielsen, F. "Hispanics in High School and Beyond." In M. A. Olivas (ed.), *Latino College Students.* New York: Teachers College Press, 1986.

Olivas, M. A. *The Dilemma of Access.* Washington, D.C.: Howard University Press, 1979.

Orfield, G., and others. *Chicago Study of Access and Choice in Higher Education.* Chicago: Chicago Committee on Public Policy Studies Research Project, University of Chicago, 1984.

Parsons, T., and Platt, G. M. *The American University.* Cambridge, Mass.: Harvard University Press, 1973.

Pennock-Roman, M. "Fairness in the Use of Tests for Selective Admissions of Hispanics." In M. A. Olivas (ed.), *Latino College Students.* New York: Teachers College Press, 1986.

Richardson, R. C., Jr., and Bender, L. W. *Students in Urban Settings: Achieving the Baccalaureate Degree.* ASHE-ERIC Higher Education Report, no. 6. Washington, D.C.: Association for the Study of Higher Education, 1985.

Richardson, R. C., Jr., and Bender, L. W. *Helping Minorities Achieve Degrees: The Urban Connection.* Tempe: National

Center for Postsecondary Governance and Finance, Research Center at Arizona State University, 1986.

Richardson, R. C., Jr., and Doucette, D. S. *Persistence, Performance, and Degree Achievement of Arizona Community College Transfers in Arizona's Public Universities.* Tempe: Arizona State University, 1980.

Richardson, R. C., Jr., Fisk, E. C., and Okun, M. A. *Literacy in the Open-Access College.* San Francisco: Jossey-Bass, 1983.

Rudnick, A. J., edited by N. Brown. *The American University in the Urban Context: A Status Report and Call for Leadership.* Washington, D.C.: National Association of State Universities and Land-Grant Colleges, 1983.

Santos, R. "Hispanic High School Graduates: Making Choices." In M. A. Olivas (ed.), *Latino College Students.* New York: Teachers College Press, 1986.

Schein, E. H. *Organizational Culture and Leadership: A Dynamic View.* San Francisco: Jossey-Bass, 1985.

Smartt, S. H. *Urban Universities in the 80s: Issues and Statewide Planning.* Atlanta, Ga.: Southern Regional Education Board, 1981.

University of California, Los Angeles. "Persistence and Graduation Information." Unpublished report. Los Angeles: Office of Information Management and Institutional Research, 1986.

Waetjen, W. B., and Muffo, J. A. "The Urban University: Model for Actualization." *Review of Higher Education,* 1983, *3,* 207–215.

Weiss, L. *Between Two Worlds.* Boston: Routledge & Kegan Paul, 1985.

Whiteley, M. A., and Lacy, E. C. *Demographics of Minority Student Recruitment: Arizona State University.* Tempe, Ariz.: Office of University Planning and Analysis, 1985.

Wilson, R. "Minority Students and the Community College." In L. S. Zwerling (ed.), *The Community College and Its Critics.* New Directions for Community Colleges, no. 54. San Francisco: Jossey-Bass, 1986.

Wilson, R., and Melendez, S. E. *Minorities in Higher Education: Fifth Annual Status Report.* Washington, D.C.: American Council on Education, 1986.

Index

H

I

J

K

L

M